Editor
Polly Hoffman

Editorial Project Manager
Mara Ellen Guckian

Editor-in-Chief
Sharon Coan, M.S. Ed.

Illustrators
Alexandra Artigas
Kevin Barnes
Rene Christine Yates

Cover Artist
Lesley Palmer

Art Coordinator
Kevin Barnes

Art Director
CJae Froshay

Imaging
Ralph Olmedo, Jr.

Product Manager
Phil Garcia

Publishers
Rachelle Cracchiolo, M.S. Ed.
Mary Dupuy Smith, M.S. Ed.

Practice & Assess Through the Year

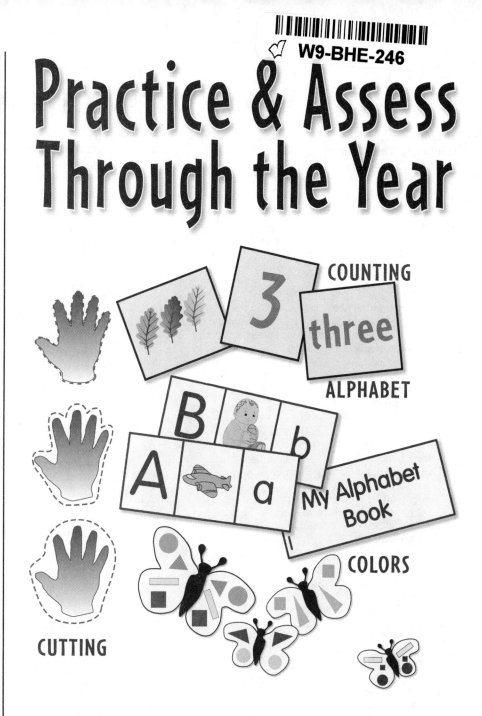

Author

Marian Weber

Teacher Created Materials, Inc.
6421 Industry Way
Westminster, CA 92683
www.teachercreated.com

ISBN-07439-3227-7

©2003 Teacher Created Materials, Inc.

Made in U.S.A.

Table of Contents

Introduction

This book is designed to help the preschool teacher measure each student's growth in the following areas:

- Scissors skills and cutting
- Color identification
- Counting
- Number identification

- Alphabet recognition
- Writing first name
- Writing last name

The evaluation and recording of these skills will help the teacher and parent follow and assist the child's progress. The repetitive nature of these pages is intentional. It is done for two reasons: The first is to make the testing uniform so growth can be measured throughout the year. The second purpose was to make it simple for both teachers and students to use without having to spend time learning a new activity each month for testing. Children's self esteem improves, too, as they recognize an activity and can see their own improvement from month to month.

A major goal in the early childhood setting is to help the child be prepared for school. Instructors work toward social, emotional, and developmental growth. This book is intended to observe developmental growth in a measurable way. Of course, the challenge of working with young children is that learning is not subdivided so neatly. Keeping this in mind as you use this book, feel free to adapt the tests and expand the activities as you desire, as well as testing quarterly instead of monthly, if desired.

These pages will give you quick and easy methods to measure the students in early academic skills. Having this information will help you know where each child "is" and how "far" you need to bring him or her to be considered proficient or successful in school. The academic skills can be assessed on a monthly basis, however the assessment cards are seasonal. For example, you could test your students three times using the winter assessment cards and three in the spring.

This early childhood assessment book includes a home connection to involve parents in their child's education. When you have finished the months' assessments, the materials, along with the directions cards, can be sent home as enrichment activities for parents to use with their child. Each activity can be sent home in a resealable bag. You may wish to ask a few parents to help you prepare each month's assessment materials. This will further the home-school connection and save you valuable time!

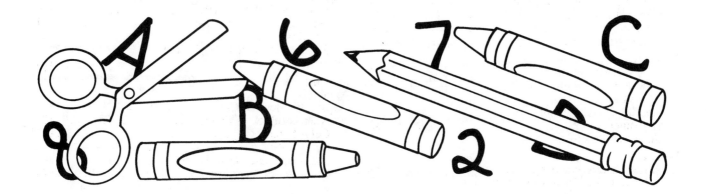

How to Use This Book

Remember as you assess your students, each child, each teacher, and each school's curriculum is different. Use this book as a tool to help you gather and record information about each of your students. In turn, this information will help you get to know each of your students and meet their individual needs while staying within the parameters of your school and district curriculum guidelines.

Incorporate these activities in your lesson plans at the end of each month. Plan one to two days for each area of assessment. Adjust the amount of time needed in relationship to the number of children in the class. Initially, plan approximately 15 to 20 minutes for each group of five children. As the year progresses, your students will become more familiar with the assessment activities and less time will be necessary for them. The children will not need as many directions to complete the tasks.

To begin, divide students into groups of three to five children. Put children at similar levels in the same group. The groups may need to change for each skill assessed because children have varied strengths and weaknesses. Be sure that the remaining students in the class are engaged in an activity that will keep them occupied while you work with each group.

Day one of assessments is used to measure cutting skills. Page 8 contains information on cutting and how to determine each child's cutting level.

On the second day, students will be assessed on their ability to identify and name specific colors. Over the course of a few months, more and more children will have mastered color identification. When this occurs, it is not necessary to test such students on this specific skill. Assessments can be moved to the next phase by changing the color shapes to color words.

Academic skill assessments (math and colors) may take more time than cutting skills because it is important to have the children demonstrate their knowledge by repeating the process two or three times. There are different assessment cards for each season. Depending on the number of times you want to assess your students, you may use the fall cards in September, October, or November.

There are two options for recording the assessment. Individual Student Assessment Forms for each student are on page 143. You can copy one for each child and then record on the forms as you work with the individual in a small group. This information is helpful in understanding how each student is performing and useful when conferencing with parents.

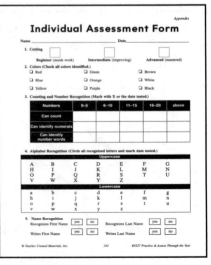

A second form is available on page 144. This is the Group Assessment Form. This form allows you to record each child's results on one form. When completed, the form will give an overview of how your class is doing as a whole. This will enable you to adjust your lessons to suit the ever-changing needs of your class.

If possible, use both the individual and the complete class assessment forms. Transfer the information from the individual form to the complete class form so that you can see both individual and class results. It works well to use a three-ring notebook to help with organization. Keep the class assessment form at the beginning of the notebook, followed by the individual student forms.

Planning Time for Assessments

Day One—Cutting Assessment

- Copy an Individual Assessment Form for each child.
- Prepare, for each child, the materials listed on page 7 for the cutting assessment.
- Have students complete the cutting project.
- Record results on the assessment form. (Use assessment guidelines on p. 8)

Day Two—Color Assessment

- Prepare, for each child, the color shapes and picture mat listed on the color assessment.
- Play the activity with one to five children using the color shapes and activity mats.
- Record the colors identified by each child on the Individual Assessment Form.
- Give each child a resealable bag containing a copy of the parent directions and materials needed for parents to work on the activity with their child.

Days Three and Four—Math Assessment

- Prepare the number flash cards for each child.
- Play the activity with one to five children. Adjust the activity to the developmental level of the child(ren) with whom you are working.
- Record the counting level or numbers identified on the Assessment Form.
- In a resealable bag, send home a copy of the parent directions and materials needed for parents to work on the activity with their child.

Days Five and Six—Alphabet Assessment

- Prepare a copy of the alphabet game sheet and cards for each child.
- Play the activity with one to five children. Adjust the activity to the developmental level of the child(ren) with whom you are working.
- Record the letters identified on the Individual Assessment Form.
- In a resealable bag, send home a copy of the parent directions and materials needed for parents to work on the activity with their child.

Day Seven—Writing Name Assessment

- Copy a Name Writing page for each child.
- Have the child write his or her first name. Once the first name is mastered, begin working on the last name.
- Record the results on the Individual Assessment Form.

Learning to Use Scissors

At first glance, cutting skills seem pretty simple, but put scissors in the hands of three-year-olds and the challenges become quite clear. A child's ability to cut accurately depends on his or her muscle development. Many children need to strengthen their hand muscles before attempting to cut paper.

Developing hand muscles (fine motor skills) can be done with simple finger plays, especially those requiring the child to open and close his or her fingers. Other entertaining activities to help develop fine motor skills include:

- Squeezing clay
- Wringing out wet sponges
- Using clothespins
- Picking up items with tongs and tweezers
- Using plastic eyedroppers to drip colored water into ice cube trays or onto coffee filters

Working with Scissors

✄ *Which hand does the child use?*

Not all children will have a preference on which hand to use. The earliest a child will show some hand dominance is about the age of three, but most children don't show a real preference until around kindergarten age. Allow the child to choose which hand he or she prefers. It may change from one hand to the other, even during a single cutting project.

✄ *What type of scissors should be used?*

There are many types of child friendly scissors from which to choose. Many are made specifically for children. Try to purchase scissors that can be used in either the left or the right hand and have plastic or rubber grips. Always buy scissors with rounded tips to prevent accidents.

How should the scissors be held?

✄ Explain to your students that they need to keep their thumbs up. Teach each child to put his or her thumb in the little hole and the other fingers in the larger hole. Depending on the size of the child's fingers, he or she may place two or three fingers in the large opening.

How should the child start cutting?

✄ After the child has his or her fingers placed correctly in the scissors' handles, explain to him or her that it is important to keep his or her thumb up. For many children, it helps to call the place where the material is being cut as the the "V" of the scissors. Ask the child to put the paper all the way to the V and squeeze up and down, using the handles.

Cutting Practice

Safety Rules

1. When carrying the scissors, hold them like a bunch of flowers. Hold the stems (shaft) with the flowers (handles) showing on the top.

2. Walk, don't run, when carrying scissors.

3. Only cut things you have permission to cut.

Procedure

When it is cutting time, take down the scissors and supplies, and review the safety rules. Allow the children to experience cutting at their own pace. Place one to three children on the floor around a plastic tub or shoebox filled with the materials to be cut. To maintain interest, change the materials from time to time.

Some suggested materials include:

- construction paper
- junk mail
- paint chips
- wallpaper

- drinking straws
- newspaper
- cards
- wax paper

- foil
- old greeting cards
- play dough
- sandpaper

Beginner

Children just learning to cut will need to work on holding the scissors correctly, as well as holding the paper appropriately. To give the beginner experience, gather cutting supplies in a plastic tub or shoebox and work with a small group of children at a time.

Intermediate

Intermediate cutters can continue practicing their skills by cutting a variety of items. Change the items in the cutting box to include both straight and wavy lines to cut. Also include simple shapes, pages of pretend money, and pictures from catalogs.

Advanced

Advanced cutters are ready for cutting out more intricate shapes. Provide these students with opportunities to practice cutting out both large and small shapes on one piece of paper. The shapes should be increasingly more complex with more curves and corners.

Recording Monthly Cutting Assessments

When assessing each student, consider the **process**—How did the session go while the child was cutting?

- Did the child often ask for help?
- Did the child know how to start and complete the assignment?

When assessing each student, consider the **project**—How successful was the end result?

- Did the child cut on the lines?
- Was there much tearing or ripping of the paper?
- Did the child maintain the original shape?

Cutting Skills

Mark beginner if:

○ The teacher traces around the child's hand without finger indentions, creating a single closed shape.

○ The child chops at the paper and has trouble holding the paper with the other hand as well as forgetting finger positions in the scissors.

○ The cutting was random, not always on the lines. It does not look like the complete shape and may be torn.

Mark intermediate if:

○ The teacher and the student work together to trace the student's hand.

○ The child understands staying on the cutting line but has some trouble turning the paper for curves and corners.

○ The shape is recognizable but may have parts accidentally cut or torn.

Mark advanced if:

○ The students traces his or her hand without assistance.

○ The child stays on the cutting lines and turns the paper with his or her other hand to cut curves and corners.

○ The final shape matches the one that was traced.

Writing Our Names

Teaching a child to write his or her name is an important step toward kindergarten readiness. To do this seemingly simple task will require the preschool child to develop five specific components. These are visual motor skills, visual perception, fine motor skills, trunk control, and shoulder stability. Here are basic definitions of these skills and suggestions on how to increase the child's development in each area.

Visual Motor Skills
This phase has to do with the eye-hand connection. It is the ability to look at something and then have the hand do what the brain is telling it to do.

Practice
- Drawing a line from one object to another, following a dotted line, or tracing shapes with a finger, crayon, marker, or pencil, are all ways to develop this skill.

> **Teacher Tip:** Gripping the pencil will vary among children. The thumb and first finger should form an oval when holding a pencil.

Visual Perception
This phase has to do with how a student understands what he or she sees. An example would be understanding the difference between the letters "b" and "p."

Practice
- Letter and shape recognition games
- Using tangrams and pattern blocks
- Completing age-appropriate puzzles

> **Teacher Tip:** Remind your students to *use both hands* when writing; one holds the pencil and one holds the paper.

Fine Motor Control
This phase deals with the child's hand muscles. The child needs to be able to pinch the thumb and first finger together, curl the fingers in toward the palm, as well as using his or her pinky finger side of the hand for strength and balance.

Practice
- Tearing paper, construction paper, or clay
- Stringing beads
- Completing lacing cards
- Picking up small objects with tongs and tweezers

> **Teacher Tip:** *A thick pencil is a good writing utensil* for small hands to use. If a student has trouble holding a pencil, he or she may not be developmentally ready to write.

Trunk Control
This phase has to do with the child's ability to support him or herself physically while writing. A child with poor trunk control will lean his or her head, arm, or body on the table. The child is not physically strong enough to maintain the posture needed for writing.

Practice
- Animal walks where child's hands and feet are on the floor (crab, cow, bear, etc.)
- Activities done with the tummy on the floor, such as coloring, will strengthen the back muscles.

Shoulder Stability
This phase deals with the necessary strength of the shoulder muscles. When a student writes, the movements need to be very slow and they need to have well-controlled shoulder movements.

Practice
- Standing up while drawing, coloring, or writing at a chalkboard or easel
- Stacking dominoes or blocks

Teaching Name Writing

There are several things to decide before teaching students to write their names. First, determine what style of lettering you would like the children to learn, *modern* or *traditional*. If it is possible, you may want to learn which style is being taught in the local schools. This makes for a smoother transition when your students go to kindergarten.

Modern

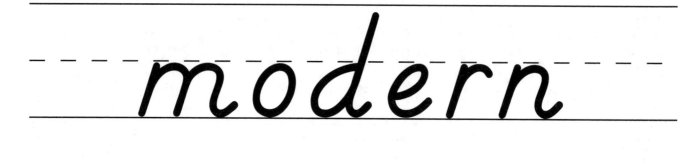

Traditional

Besides the style, you will want to decide what vocabulary to use as well. There are several different terms used for similar styles of handwriting.

Finally, you will want to decide what letter form the student will use when writing. Do you want him to write his or her name in all uppercase letters or would you prefer the first letter be capitalized and the letters that follow written in lowercase.

It is important to decide in advance so expectations will be clear for both you and your students.

The practice pages have three lines for name writing. Model for your students how to write their names by demonstrating on the first line. Then, ask your students to trace over the letters you have written. Watch closely to ensure that your students are beginning the letters at the appropriate places, as well as moving their pencils in the correct direction. The second and third lines are for your students to practice copying and writing their names.

Name Writing Assessments

At this early stage of development, the name writing assessment is complete with a simple *yes* or *no*. As students progress through the year, you should see marked improvement.

☐ Mark **yes** if the student has made all the letters of his or her name clear enough for you to read.

☐ Mark **no** if the student has not written the name correctly or clearly. The letters will not be discernable, some may be missing or other letters or marks are added.

The Modern Alphabet

The Traditional Alphabet

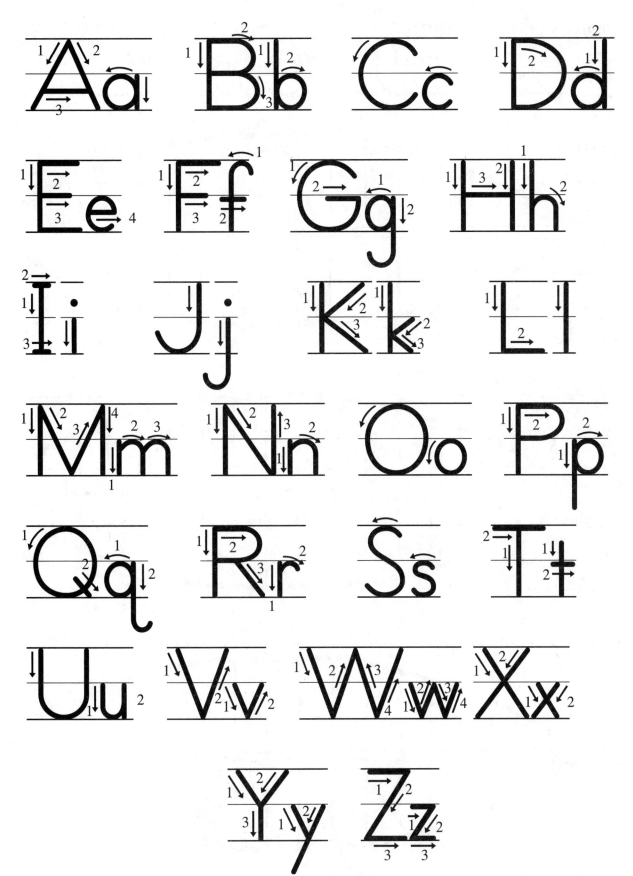

Fern Cutting Practice

Beginning Cutting Practice

Directions: Provide each child with a leaf shape. Have each child snip the short lines, using scissors, to produce a fern or pine leaf.

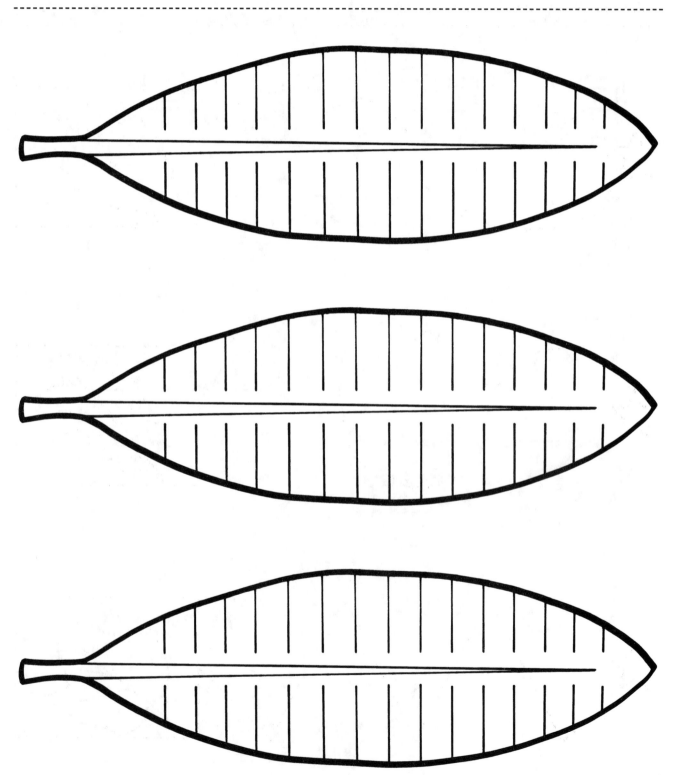

Leaf Cutting Practice

Intermediate Cutting Practice

Directions: Ask each student to begin cutting at the stars and continue to cut along the dotted line. Explain to your students that they need to continue cutting until they reach the box. Then, instruct your students to cut out the box with the leaf inside it.

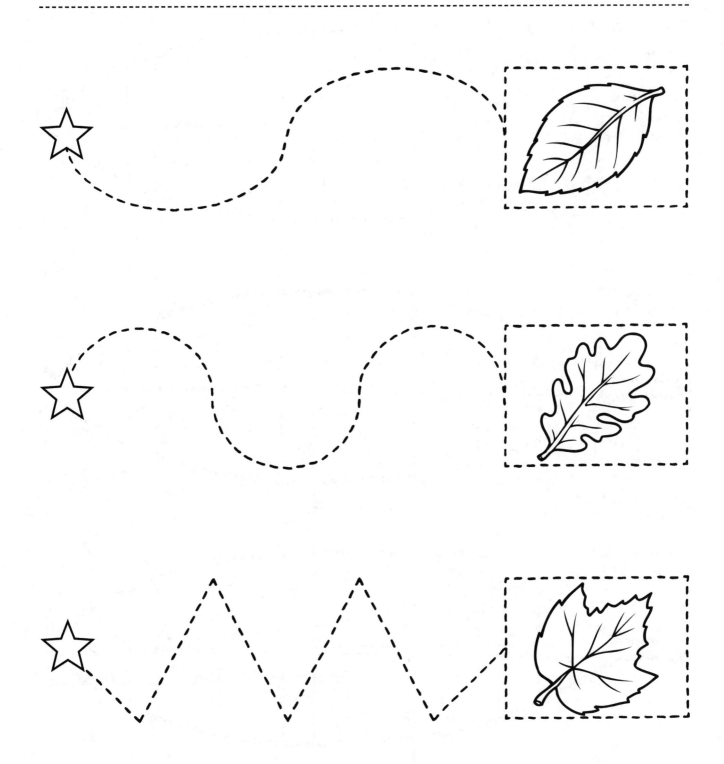

September Cutting Activity

Materials

- Pencils
- Children's safety scissors
- Red, yellow, and orange construction paper
- Tree Trunk Mat (page 19), enlarged
- Individual or Group Assessment Forms (pages 143–144)

Procedure

1. Ask your students to trace their hands on different pieces of fall-colored construction paper. Remind students to keep the hand that is on the paper still and use their other hand to move the pencil. For some children it helps to put a little piece of rolled up tape on the under side of the construction paper while tracing. This helps prevent the paper from moving.

2. When your students have finished tracing their hands, provide scissors for them to cut out the tracings. Save each child's cut-out hands to use in the culminating activity.

Assessment

Encourage children to show you the hands they cut out. Mark their skill levels on the appropriate form: *beginner, intermediate,* or *advanced.* Refer to the Cutting Skills on page 8 for guidelines.

Culminating Activity

Enlarge or trace the tree trunk pattern on brown paper to fit the display area or bulletin board. Cut out the trunk. If only white paper was available, lay the trunk on a large table or floor and have the students color it brown. Crumple up the brown paper trunk and then spread it out again. The crumpling will create ridges similar to bark.

Attach the tree trunk to the bulletin board and add the hand-shaped leaves your students made. Encourage your students to point to where they want their leaves to be placed on the tree using directional words like above, below, and beside.

Sample Bulletin Board Design

Fall Color Identification

Materials

- Leaf Patterns (page 18) in red, yellow, blue, green, orange, purple, pink, brown, black, and white for each child
- Tree Trunk Mat (page 19) traced, cut, or copied, for each child
- Resealable bag for each child
- Individual or Group Assessment Forms (pages 143–144)

Procedure

Provide enough leaf shapes so that every child has two of each color. Trace, cut, or copy a tree trunk for each child. Divide the class into groups of three to five children at similar levels. Work with one small group at a time, while the remaining students are working on another independent activity.

Teacher's Note: *When students have mastered identification of the colors, begin working on reading and recognizing the color words. Use only white leaf shapes and write a different color word on each one.*

Assessment

Provide each child with a tree trunk and an assortment of colored leaves. Explain that the object of the game is to place the correct color on the tree trunk. You can do this by naming a color, rolling a color dice, or using a spinner that lands on different colors. Allow each child to have a turn and play the game two or three times. Circle the specific colors on the child's assessment form that he or she has identified correctly.

Enrichment

In a resealable bag, send home a copy of the directions, a set of leaves, and a tree trunk so each student can play the game with his or her parents.

Directions: To begin playing this game with your child, ask your child to place the leaves on the tree trunk as you call out a color. Continue until all the colored leaves have been placed on the tree. The object of this game is to help your child learn, recognize, and identify different colors.

Leaf Patterns

Directions: Use with the tree pattern on page 19 to do color activities.

Tree Trunk Mat

1. Trace, cut, or copy the tree trunk mat to use with the colored leaves for assessment and enrichment. After assessment, send the tree trunk home with the colored leaves to use with the parent activity.

2. Enlarge the tree trunk to make a bulletin board pattern for the culminating activity.

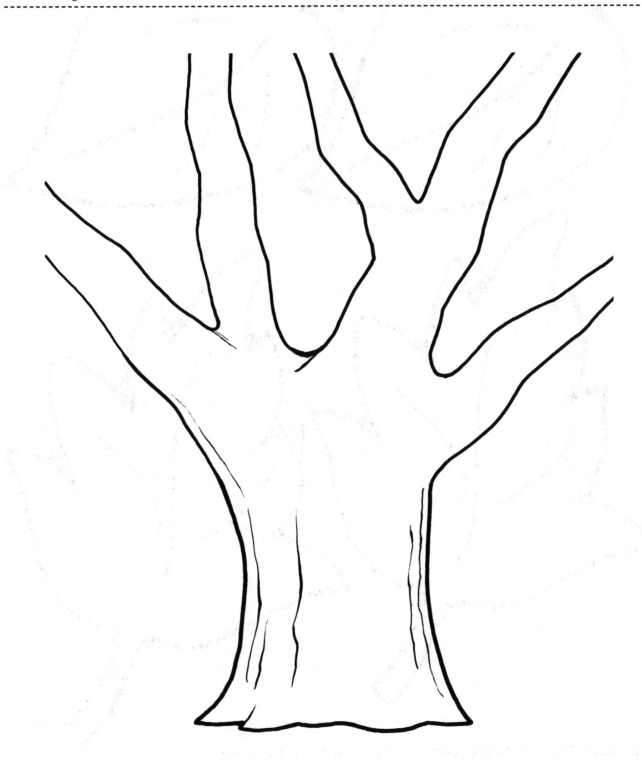

Fall Counting Activity

Materials

- Fall Counting Cards (pages 21–24) for each student
- Number Cards (pages 126–131) for each student
- Resealable bag for each student
- Individual or Group Assessment Forms (pages 143–144)

Procedure

Ask a small group of children to sit with you on the floor. Begin by giving each member of the group a copy of the Fall Counting Cards and ask them to lay the cards face up in front of them on the floor. Ask the students to hold up a card showing a certain number of leaves. You can state a specific number, have each child take a turn rolling a dice, or use a spinner that lands on the numbers you are testing. (You can adapt the spinner on page 141. Cut off or white out the color words.) Do this to practice recognizing the number amounts that each group needs to work on. Start with small amounts and add larger amounts as the students advance. Make a note on the assessment forms of those students who can recognize and count the correct number of leaves. Assess number identification and number word identification in the same way.

Teacher's Note: *Write the appropriate number on the back of each card for self-checking. Use these assessment pages in October and November as well.*

Enrichment

Send home a set of number cards, counting cards, and a copy of the activity directions. Choose cards that are appropriate for each child's level. Use resealable bags for the materials.

Directions: Begin with the counting (picture) cards. Ask your child to lay the cards out in front of him or her on the floor. Say a number and ask your child pick up the card with the same number of leaves on it. Practice all the numbers in this manner. This activity will help your child learn to count. Next, ask your child to identify the written numbers. Finally, help him or her read the number words.

Fall Counting Cards

Fall Counting Cards *(cont.)*

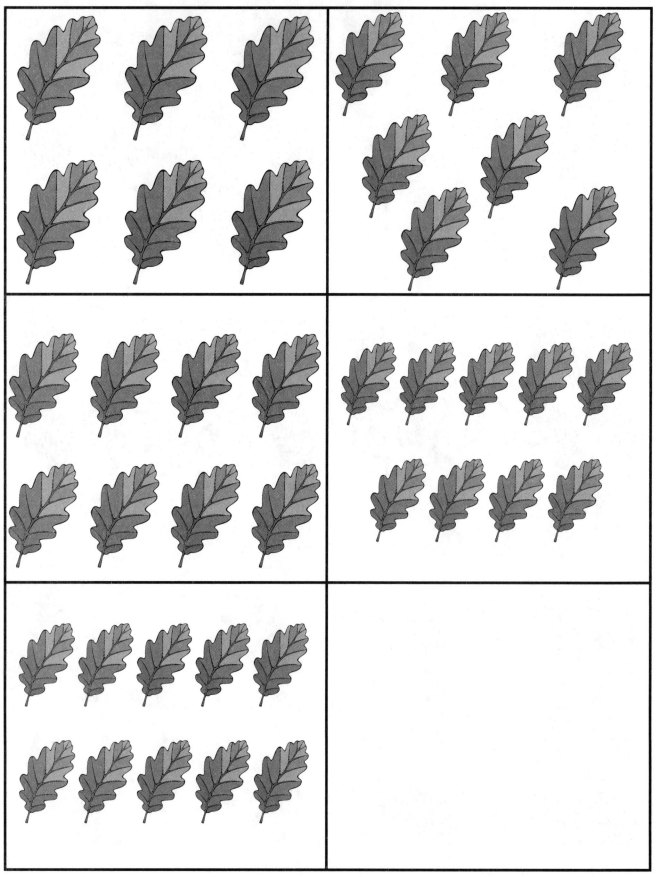

Fall Counting Cards *(cont.)*

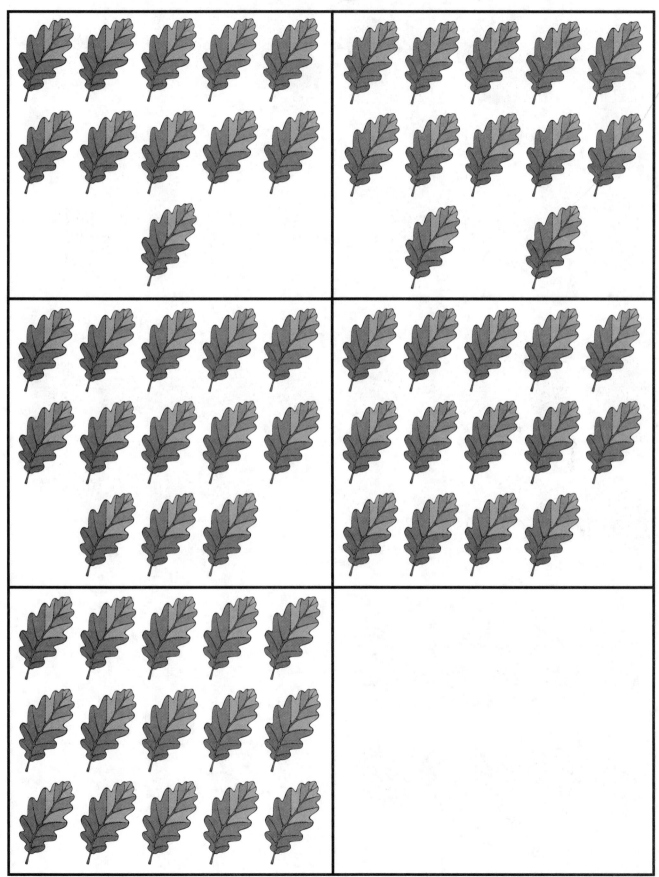

Fall Counting Cards *(cont.)*

Fall Alphabet Games

The Fall Alphabet Cards (pages 26–28) can be used in two ways, as game sheets or as flash cards. Directions for both are given below.

Game Sheets

Materials

- Fall Alphabet Cards page for each student (do not cut up)
- Markers (beans, chips, paper clips, etc.)
- Resealable bag for each student
- Individual or Group Assessment Forms (pages 143–144)

Assessment

Give each child in a small group a set of alphabet pages. Decide ahead of time if they should do all three pages at once or do them one at a time. Call out a letter in random order, and have each student find that letter on his or her sheet and cover it with a marker. This can be done as a whole group, or one at a time, giving each child a turn. Mark, on the assessment form for each child, the letters he or she child recognizes.

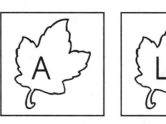

Flash Cards

Materials

- Fall Alphabet cards for each student.
- Resealable bag for each student.
- Brown paper lunch sack for each student.
- Individual or Group Assessment Forms (page 143–144)

Assessment

Mark, on the assessment form for each student, the letters he or she recognizes when cards are shown.

Enrichment

Send home the appropriate Fall Alphabet Cards in a resealable bag. Enclose a copy of the direction card below.

Raise It High Game

Ask your child to lay his or her cards on the floor in front of him or her. Name a letter of the alphabet (not in order) and ask him or her to find that card and hold it up in the air.

Letter Surprise Game

Give your child a lunch sack with the letter flash cards inside. Have him or her pull out a letter and name it. Continue until all the cards are gone.

Fall Alphabet Cards

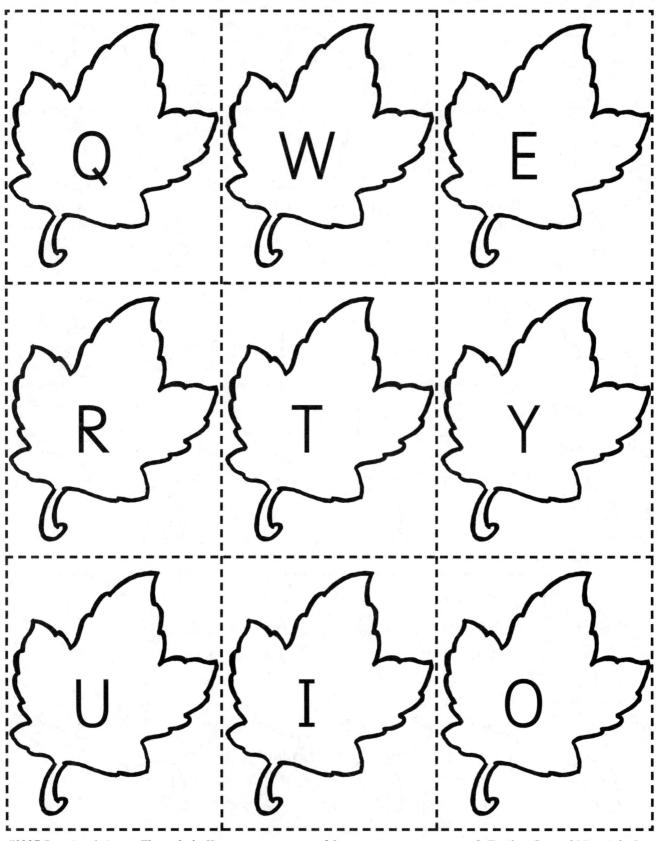

Fall Alphabet Cards *(cont.)*

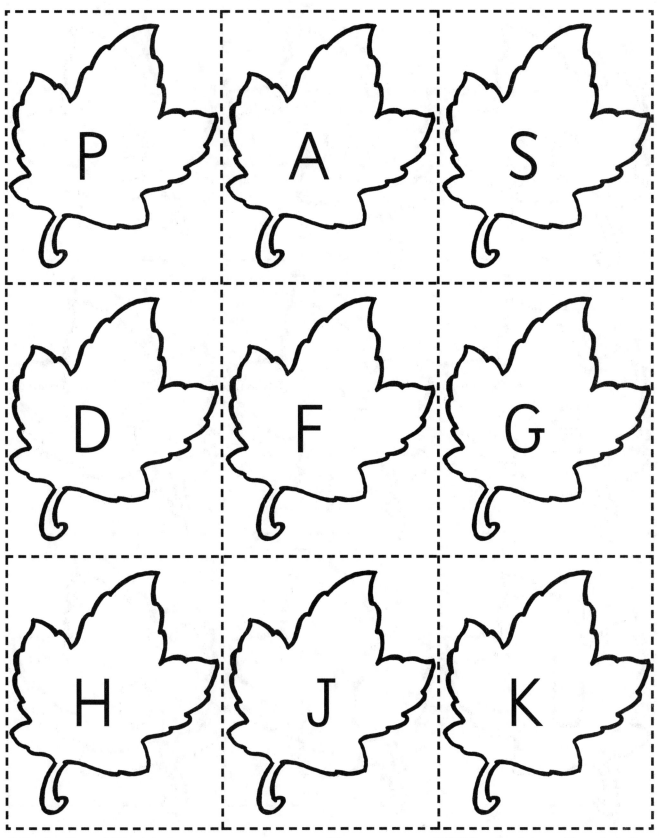

Fall Alphabet Cards *(cont.)*

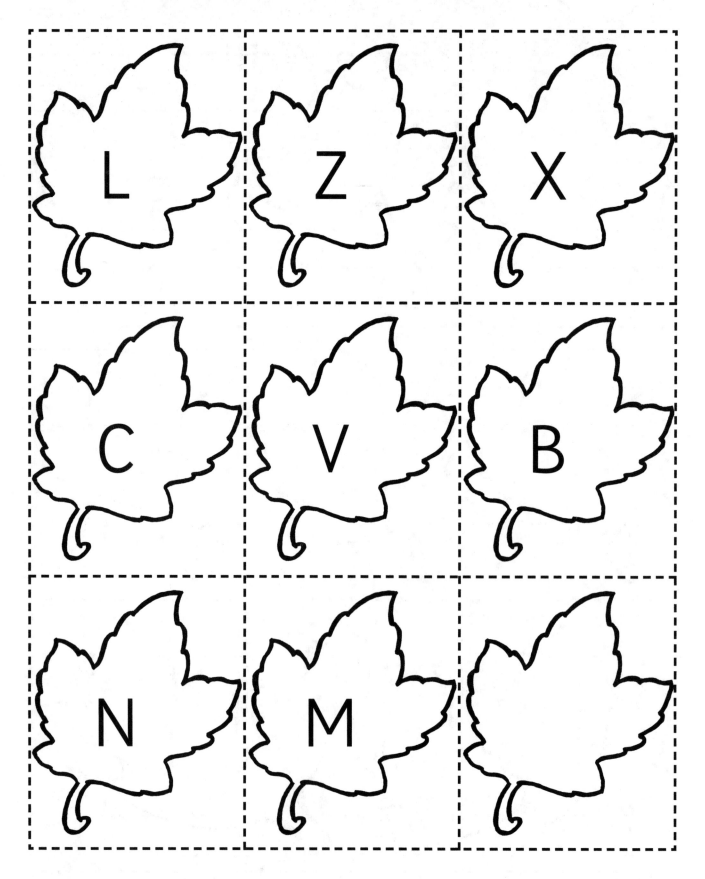

Fall Name Writing

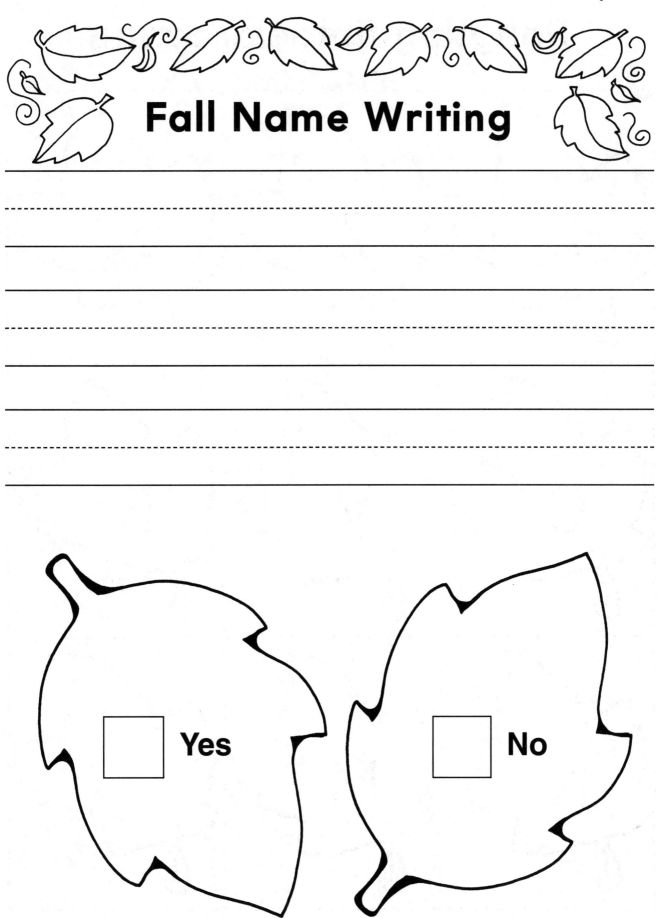

☐ Yes   ☐ No

Dangling Spider Cutting Practice

Beginner

Directions: Give each child a strip with a spider on it. Beginning at the star, ask the child to shorten the path by snipping one horizontal piece off at a time until the spider is reached.

Spider Web Cutting Practice

Intermediate

Directions: Begin at the star and follow the spider by cutting along the spider web dotted line as it winds around and around.

Spider Cutting Activity

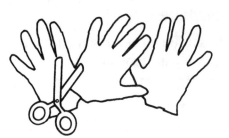

Materials

- Children's safety scissors
- 8" x 10" (20 cm x 25 cm) black construction paper
- White crayons for marking
- A pair of wiggly eyes or red circles for eyes
- Glue sticks
- Individual or Group Assessment Forms (pages 143–144)

Procedure

1. Fold black construction paper in half, horizontally so that it measures 5" x 8" (13 cm x 20 cm). Ask your students to trace, using a white crayon, their hands with the base of the palms off the folded edge. The students should curl in their thumbs, making it touch the hand. This will make a more rounded shape. The fingers need to be spread extra wide.
2. When your students have completed tracing their hands, provide scissors for them to cut them out.
3. Demonstrate for the students how to slightly bend the fingers down to make them appear to be the spider's legs.
4. Give each child a glue stick and a pair of eyes. Model for your students how to glue the eyes on top of the spider.

Assessment

Encourage children to show you their spiders. Record their levels on the appropriate cutting form: *beginner, intermediate,* or *advanced.* Refer to the Cutting Skills on page 8 for guidelines.

Culminating Activity

Make a spider web on a bulletin board or display area. Begin by covering the background with black butcher paper. Make the web by drawing on the background paper with white chalk, crayon, or paint. The web can also be made with white yarn or craft webbing material. Start the web at the center of the background and make spokes, or strait lines, move outward from this center point. After you have put in the spokes, return to the center and circularly work your way out to the edge of the web.

Attach the hand-shaped spiders to the bulletin board. Encourage the children to verbally tell you and point to where they want their spiders to be placed.

Spider Color Identification

Materials

- Spider Patterns (page 34) two of each color in red, yellow, blue, green, orange, purple, pink, brown, black, and white for each child
- Spider Web Mat (page 35) copied for each child
- Resealable bag for each child
- Individual or Group Assessment Forms (pages 143–144)

Procedure

Cut out enough spider shapes so that each child can have two of every color. Copy a spider web for each child. Divide the class into groups of three to five children who are at a similar level. Work with one group at a time, while the remaining students are working on an independent activity.

> **Teacher's Note:** *When students have mastered identification of the colors, start working on reading the color words. Practice the color words by using only white spider shapes and writing a different color name on each one.*

Assessment

Give each child a spider web mat and the assortment of colored spiders that they each made. Explain that the object of the game is to place the correct color on the spider web. Name a specific color or roll a die that has different colored sides. Give each child several turns by playing the game two or three times. When each child selects the color that has been named, circle the color on his or her assessment form.

Enrichment

In a resealable bag, send home the spiders, the web, and a copy of the directions below.

Directions: Ask your child to place the web on the floor in front of him or her and the colored spiders on the floor around it. You call out a color word and your child must place the spider of that color on the web. Continue until all colored spiders have been placed on the web. When playing this game, your child is practicing the skill of recognizing colors.

Spider Patterns

Spider Web Mat

Directions:

1. Copy the spider web pattern for each child to use with the colored spiders when doing the assessment and enrichment activities. After assessment, send the spider web home with the colored spiders.

2. Enlarge the spider web to make a bulletin board pattern for the culminating activity.

Feather Cutting Practice

Beginner

Directions: Provide each child with a precut feather piece. Using scissors, have each child snip the short, slanted, lines to produce a fluffy feather.

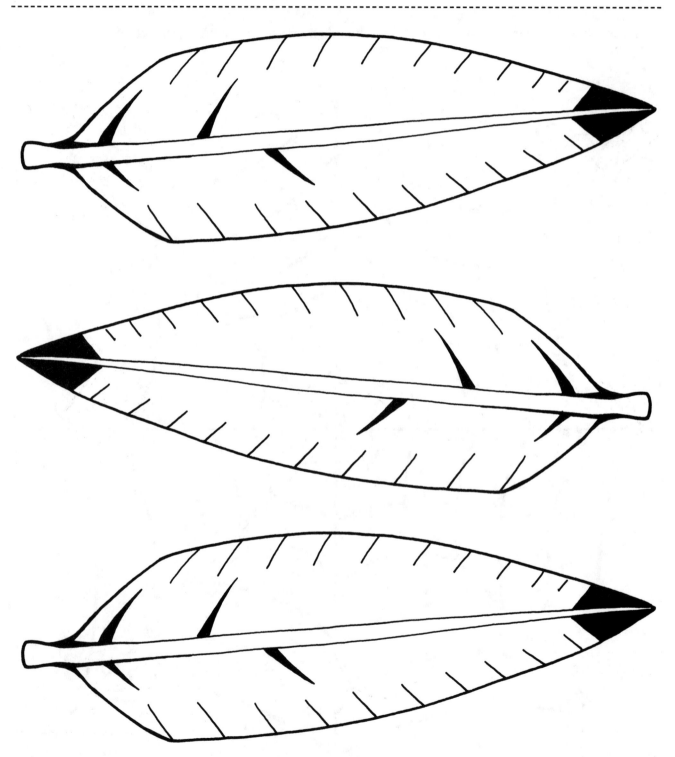

Turkey Trot Cutting Practice

Intermediate

Directions: Beginning at the stars, follow the paths of the turkeys doing the turkey trot with your scissors. Cut along the path until the turkey at the end is reached. Have each child practice three times.

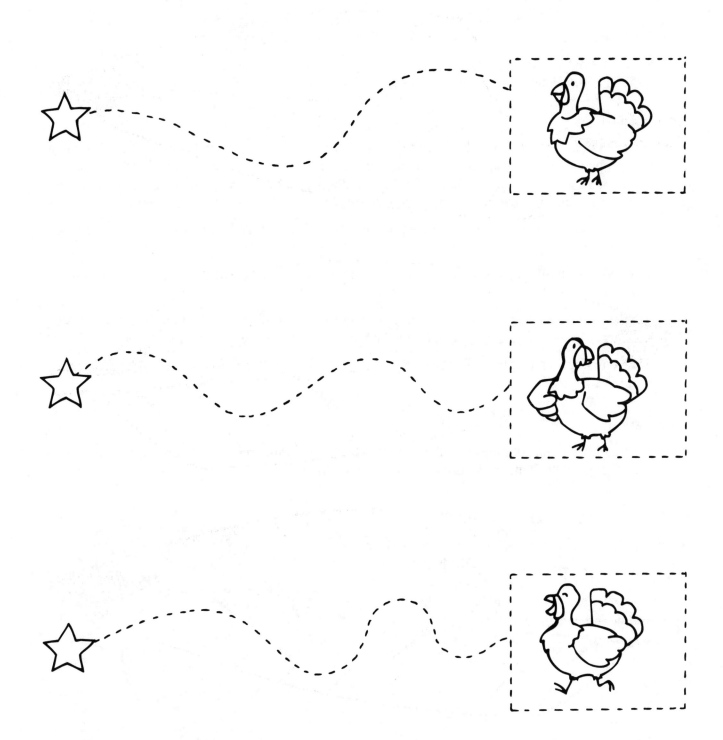

November Cutting Activity

Materials

- Pencils
- Children's safety scissors
- Brown construction paper for turkey
- Green construction paper for background
- Glue sticks
- Crayons and/or colored feathers
- Individual or Group Assessment Forms (page 143–144)

Procedure

1. Have children trace their hands on the brown construction paper. Remind each student that when tracing, he or she will want to keep the hand that is on the paper still and use their other hand to move the pencil. For some children it helps to put a little piece of rolled up tape on the underside of the construction paper during the tracing process to keep the paper from moving.

2. When your students have finished tracing their hands, give each child a pair of scissors to cut out his or her hand.

3. The children should then glue their brown hand shapes to the center of the green construction paper.

4. With crayons, tell your students to color an eye and a beak at the tip of the thumb. Next, ask your students to draw two turkey legs under the body (palm of the hand) of the turkey.

5. Ask your students to color the fingers of the turkey to represent the tail feathers. Real feathers could also be used.

Assessment

Mark each child's cutting skill level on the cutting assessment form: *beginner, intermediate,* or *advanced.* Refer to the Cutting Skills on page 8 for guidelines.

Culminating Activity

Make a turkey body and head out of brown construction paper or brown butcher paper. Cut the body and head out and attach it to a bulletin board. Attach construction paper hands your students made to the back of the turkey to represent the turkey's tail feathers.

Feather Color Identification

Materials

- Feather Patterns (page 40) in red, yellow, blue, green, purple, pink, brown, black, and white for each child
- Turkey Mat (page 41) traced, cut, or copied, for each child
- Resealable bag for each child
- Individual or Group Assessment Forms (pages 143–144)

Procedure

Cut enough feather shapes so that each child has two of every color. Trace, cut, or copy a turkey pattern for each child. Divide the class into groups of three to five children that are at similar developmental levels. Work with one small group of children at a time, while the remaining students in the class are working independently.

> **Teacher's Note:** *When students have mastered identification of colors, begin to work on reading the color words. Write each color word on a white feather shape.*

Assessment

Give each child a turkey and his or her assortment of colored feather shapes. Explain to your students that the object of the game is to place the correct color feather on the turkey. The teacher names a specific color and the student(s) place that color feather on the turkey. Give each child a turn or play the game as a group. Play the game two or three times. When each child selects the color that has been named, circle the color on his or her assessment form.

Enrichment

In a resealable bag, send home the feather shapes, the turkey, and a copy of the game directions below.

Directions: Ask your child to place the turkey and the feather shapes on the floor in front of him or her. As you call out a color, your child then picks that color feather and places it on the turkey. Continue until all the colored feathers have been placed on the turkey. This game provides practice in recognizing color words.

Feather Patterns

Turkey Mat

Directions: Provide each student with a copy of the turkey pattern below, to use with the feather color assessment.

Snipping Wreath Cutting Practice

Beginner

Directions: Copy and cut out a wreath shape for each child. First, have the child color the wreath green and the bow red, using crayons. Next, ask each child to snip the short lines around the shape using his or her scissors. Show the child how to curl the cut ends around a crayon or pencil to give it a three-dimensional effect.

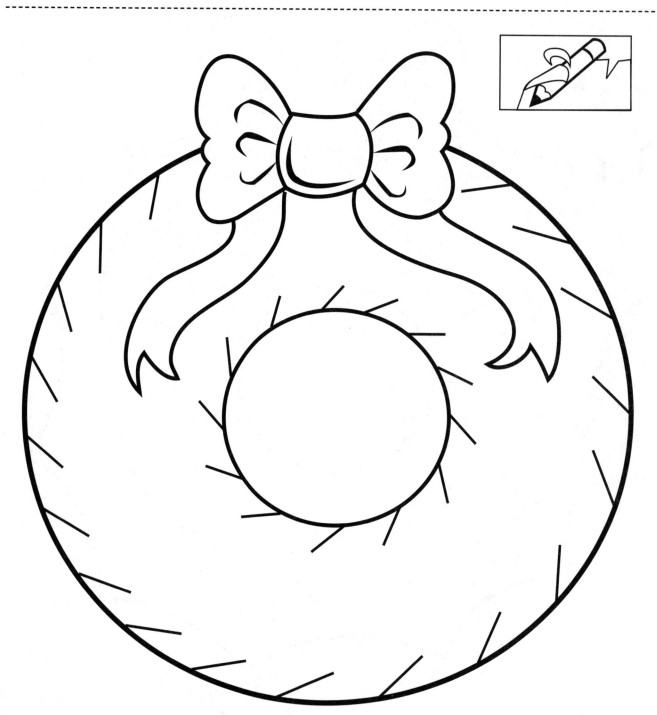

Wreath Cutting Practice

Intermediate

Directions: Give each child a copy of the wreath shape. Ask your students to color and cut out the shape. When cutting the center, show the children how to make a small fold in the middle, cut on the fold, then open it up and cut around the circle.

Hand Wreath Cutting Activity

Materials

- Pencils
- Children's safety scissors
- Green construction paper
- Red bow
- Individual or Group Assessment Forms (page 143–144)

Procedure

1. Have children trace their hands on the green piece of construction paper. Remind each student to keep the hand that is on the paper still and use his or her other hand to move the pencil. For some children, it helps to put a little piece of rolled up tape on the underside of the construction paper during the tracing process to keep the paper from moving.

2. When your students have finished tracing their hands, provide scissors for each of them to cut out the hands they traced.

Teacher's Note: *Ask each student to make several hand shapes so there are enough hands to form a wreath.*

Assessment

Encourage children to show you the hands they cut out. Mark each child's skill level on the appropriate form: *beginner, intermediate,* or *advanced.* Refer to the Cutting Skills on page 8 for guidelines.

Culminating Activity

Attach the hand shapes in a circular pattern, and overlapping, onto a bulletin board. Some of the fingers should point to the outside of the ring and some of the fingers should point to the inside of the ring. Curl and scrunch the fingers to give the wreath a three-dimensional appearance.

44

Bow Color Identification

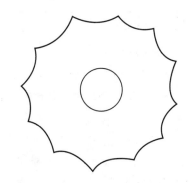

Materials

- Bow Patterns (page 46) in red, yellow, blue, green, orange, purple, pink, brown, black, and white for each child
- Wreath Mat (page 47) copied and cut out for each child
- Resealable bag for each child
- Individual or Group Assessment Forms (page 143–144)

Procedure

Cut enough bow shapes so that each child can have two of every color. Copy and cut out a wreath pattern for each child. Divide your class into groups of three to five children that are at similar levels. Work with one group at a time, while the remaining students are working independently.

Teacher's Note: *When students have mastered identification of the colors, begin to work on reading the color words. Write a different color word on several white bows.*

Assessment

Give each child a wreath and their assortment of colored bows. Explain to your students that the object of the game is to place the correct color bow on the wreath. The teacher names a specific color and the student(s) place that color bow on the wreath. Give each child several turns by playing the game two or three times. As each child selects the color that has been named, circle the color on his or her assessment form.

Enrichment

In a resealable bag, send home the bows, the wreath, and a copy of the directions below. Parents can then work on the skill of color recognition at home.

Directions: Play the following color recognition game with your child. Ask your child to place the bows and the wreath on the floor in front of him or her. Name a specific color and ask your child to find that color bow and place it on the wreath. Continue until all the colored bows have been placed on the wreath. This game provides practice in recognizing colors.

Bow Patterns

Wreath Mat

Directions: Copy and cut out the wreath pattern to use with the colored bow patterns for assessment and enrichment. When done assessing your students, send the wreath and the colored bows home with your students so they can play the game with a parent.

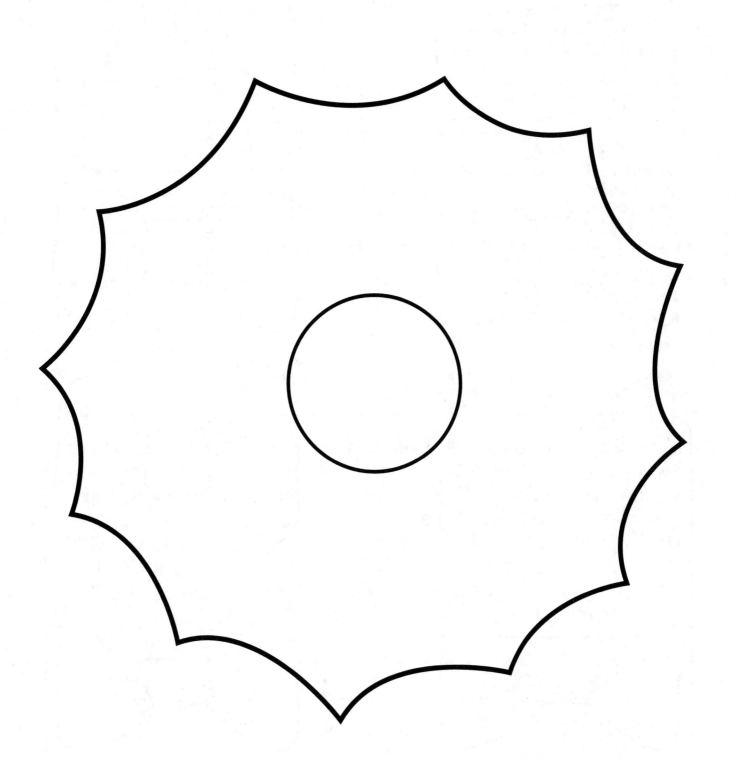

Winter Counting Activities

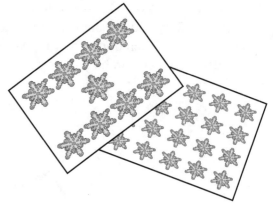

Materials

- Winter Counting Cards (pages 49–52) for each student
- Number Cards (pages 126–131) for each student
- Resealable bag for each student
- Individual or Group Assessment Forms (pages 143–144)

Procedure

Prepare a set of the Winter Counting Cards for each student in your group. Ask your students to lay them out on the floor in front of them. Ask the group members to hold up a card displaying a certain number of snowflakes. State a specific number, or use another means to come up with a number on which your group is working. Try rolling a die or using a spinner. Do this to practice recognizing the numbers that are appropriate for each group. Start with small numbers and add larger numbers as the students advance. Record on each child's assessment form the numbers he or she can count and identify correctly. Assess number identification and number word identification in the same way.

Teacher's Note: *Add the appropriate number to the back of each card for self-checking. Use these assessment pages in January and February as well.*

Enrichment

Send home a set of number cards, counting cards, and a copy of the directions below. Place them in a resealable bag. Choose cards that are appropriate for each child's individual level.

Directions: Play the following number game with your child. Ask your child to lay his or her counting (picture) cards on the floor in front of him or her. Say a number and have your child pick up the card that represents that number of snowflakes. Repeat this activity until your child has practiced all numbers. This game will help your child learn to count. Next, ask your child to identify the written numbers. Finally, help him or her practice reading the number words.

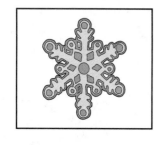  

Winter Counting Cards

Winter Counting Cards *(cont.)*

Winter Counting Cards (cont.)

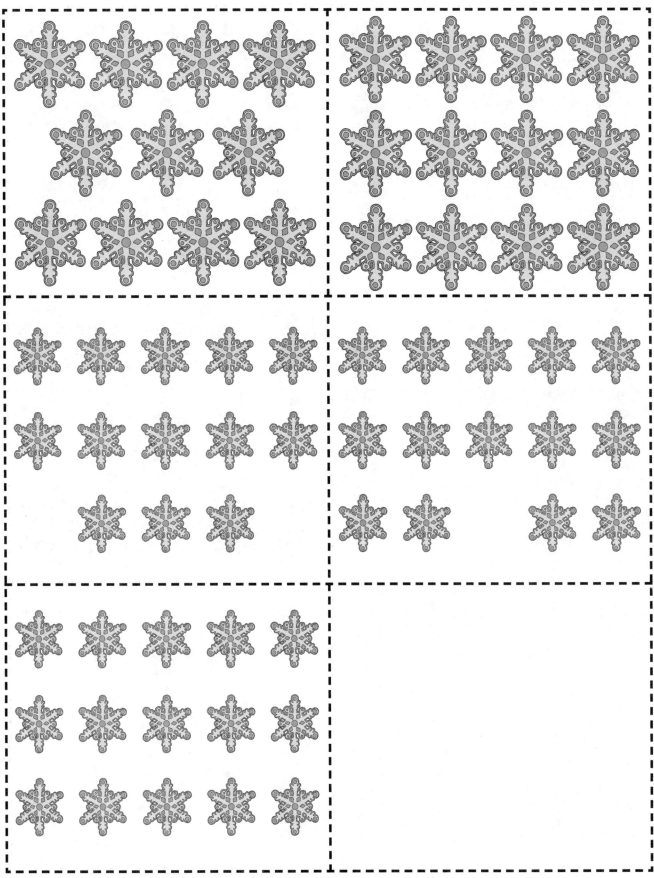

Winter Counting Cards *(cont.)*

Winter
Counting
Cards

Winter Alphabet Games

The Winter Alphabet Cards (pages 54–56) can be used in two ways, as game sheets or as flash cards. Directions for both are given below.

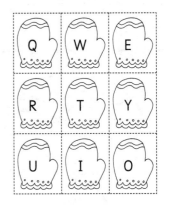

Game Sheets

Materials

- Winter Alphabet Cards for each student (do not cut up)
- Markers (beans, chips, paper clips, etc.)
- Resealable bag for each student
- Individual or Group Assessment Forms (pages 143–144)

Assessment

Give each child in a small group a set of winter alphabet pages. Decide ahead of time if they should do all three pages at once or do them one at a time. Call out a letter in random order, and have students find that letter on their sheets and cover them with a marker. This can be done as a whole group, or one at a time, giving each child a turn. Mark on the assessment form, for each individual child, the letters he or she recognizes.

Flash Cards

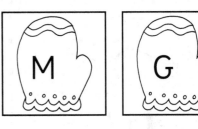

Materials

- Winter Alphabet Cards for each student
- Resealable bag for each student
- Brown paper lunch sack for each student
- Individual or Group Assessment Forms (page 143–144)

Assessment

Mark, on the assessment form for each child, the letters he or she recognizes when cards are shown.

Enrichment

Send home the appropriate Winter Alphabet Cards in a resealable bag. Enclose a copy of the direction card below.

Raise It High Game

Ask your child to lay his or her cards on the floor in front of him or her. Name a letter of the alphabet (not in order) and ask him or her to find that card and hold it up in the air.

Letter Surprise Game

Give your child a lunch sack with the letter cards inside. Have him or her pull out a letter and name it. Continue until all the cards are gone.

Winter Alphabet Cards

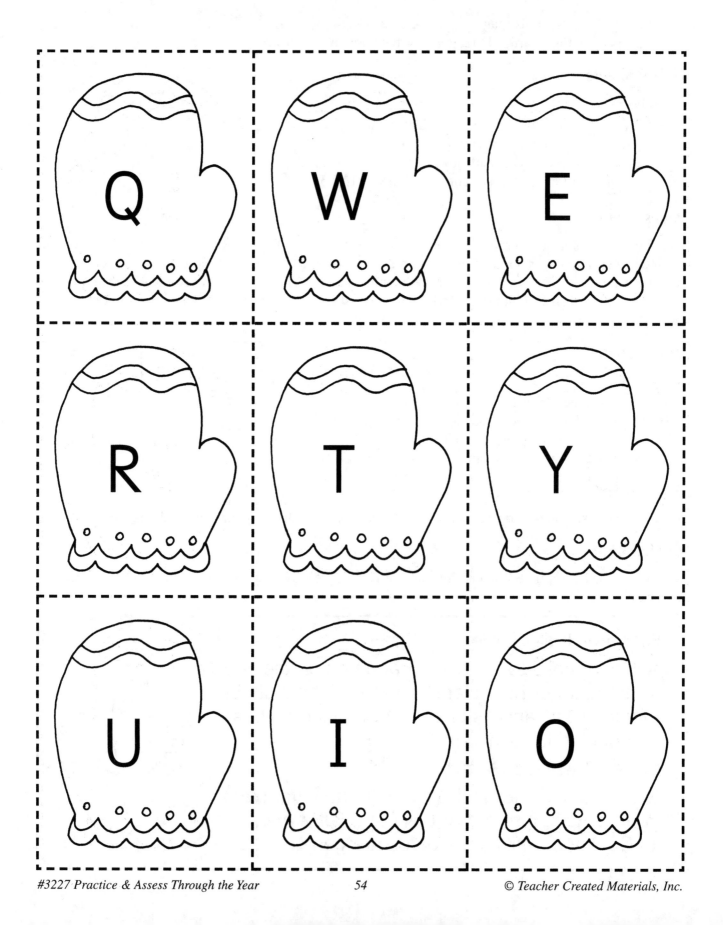

Winter Alphabet Cards *(cont.)*

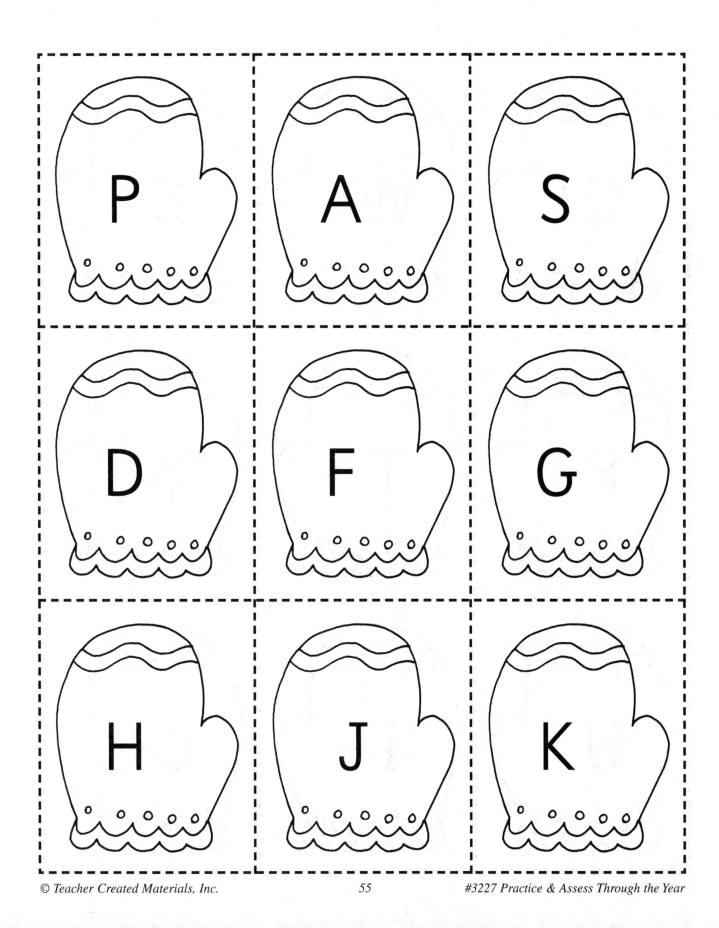

Winter Alphabet Cards *(cont.)*

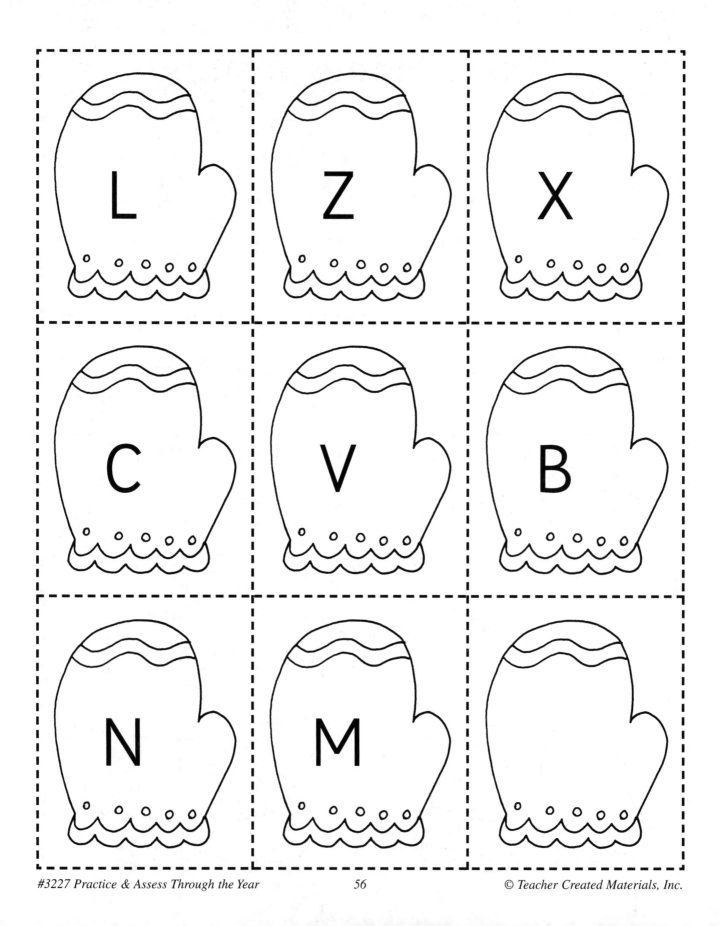

Winter Name Writing

Yes   No

Tassel Cutting Practice

Beginner

Directions: Cut out a hat shape for each child. Ask each child to decorate his or her hat using crayons or markers. When finished decorating, ask your students to snip the short lines to produce a tassel top.

Rolling Yarn Cutting Practice

Intermediate

Directions: Follow the paths of the unrolling yarn. Ask your students to begin by placing their scissors on the stars. Next, ask them to cut along the dotted lines to cut out the balls of yarn.

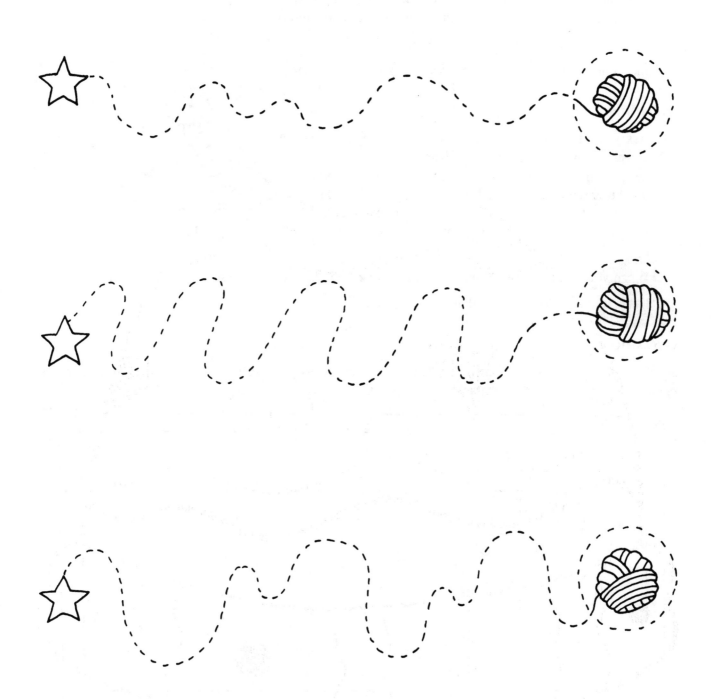

Glove Cutting Activity

Materials

- Children's safety scissors
- Pencils
- Variety of colored construction paper
- Assorted materials for the children to decorate their glove shapes, such as yarn, ribbon, sequins, glitter, stickers, and buttons.
- Glue and/or glue sticks
- Individual or Group Assessment Forms (pages 143–144)

Procedure

1. Ask your students to trace their hands on a piece of colored construction paper. Remind students, that when tracing, to keep the hand that is on the paper still and use the other hand to trace with the pencil. For some children it helps to put a little piece of rolled up tape on the underside of the construction paper to keep the paper still during the tracing process.

2. When your students have completed tracing their hands, provide scissors so they can cut them out.

3. Decorate the "gloves" once they have been cut out.

Assessment

Encourage children to show you the hands they cut out. Mark their skill levels on the appropriate form: *beginner, intermediate,* or *advanced.* Refer to the Cutting Skills on page 8 for guidelines.

Hat Color Identification

Materials

- Hat Patterns (page 62) in red, yellow, blue, green, orange, purple, pink, brown, black, and white for each child
- Snowman Pattern (page 63) copied and cut for each child
- Resealable bag for each child
- Individual or Group Assessment Forms (pages 143–144)

Procedure

Copy and cut enough hat shapes so that every child has two of each color. Copy and cut a snowman for each child. Divide the students into groups of three to five children who are at similar levels. Work with one group at a time, while the remaining students are working independently.

> **Teacher's Note:** *When students have mastered identification of the colors, begin to work on reading the color words. Write a different color name on each white hat shape.*

Assessment

Give each child a snowman and his or her assortment of colored hats. Explain that the object of the game is to place the correct color hat on the snowman. State a specific color, or use another means to come up with a color on which your group is working. Try rolling a die or using a spinner that lands on the different colors. Play the game two or three times giving each child several turns. When the child selects the correct color every time, circle those colors on his or her assessment form.

Enrichment

In a resealable bag, send home the hats, the snowman, and a copy of the directions below.

Directions: Play a color recognition game with your child. Ask your child to place the hats and the snowman on the floor in front of him or her. As you call out a color, ask your child to find that color hat and place it on the snowman's head. Continue until all the colored hats have been placed on the snowman's head. This game provides practice with color recognition.

Hat Patterns

Snowman Pattern

Directions: Provide a copy of the snowman pattern below for each child. Use the colored hats for the assessment and enrichment activities. After assessment, send the snowman pattern home, along with the colored hats, so the students can play the game with a parent.

Arrow Cutting Practice

Beginner

Directions: Copy and cut out an arrow shape for each child. Have the student use scissors to snip the end of the arrow to make it appear feathered.

Following Your Heart Cutting Practice

Intermediate

Directions: Follow the lines from the stars to the hearts. Begin cutting at the stars and cut along the dotted lines. When you get to the end of the dotted lines, cut out the three hearts.

"I Love You" Cutting Activity

Materials

- Pencils
- Children's safety scissors
- Red and pink construction paper
- Glue sticks
- A class set of small, red heart stickers
- Individual or Group Assessment Forms (pages 143–144)

Procedure

1. Ask your students to trace their hands on pink or red pieces of construction paper.

2. When they have finished tracing their hands, provide scissors for them to cut out the tracings.

3. Model for your students, how to fold the two middle fingers down toward the palm. Extend the thumb to form an "L" shape. This is how to say, "I love you" in sign language. Give each student a heart sticker to place in the palm of the cutout hand.

Assessment

Encourage children to show you the hands they cut out. Mark their skill levels on the appropriate form: *beginner, intermediate,* or *advanced.* Refer to the Cutting Skills on page 8 for guidelines.

Culminating Activity

Attach the "I Love You" hand shapes to a bulletin board in the shape of a heart. Put the words "I love you!" in the middle of the heart. Ask each student to tell you where to attach his or her heart by using words like *above, beside,* and *below.*

Heart Color Identification

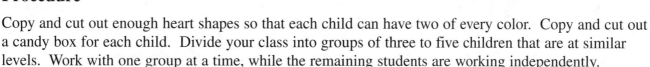

Materials

- Conversation Heart Candy Patterns (page 68) in red, yellow, blue, green, orange, purple, pink, brown, black, and white for each child
- Candy Box Mat (page 69) traced, cut, or copied, for each child
- Resealable bag for each child
- Individual or Group Assessment Forms (pages 143–144)

Procedure

Copy and cut out enough heart shapes so that each child can have two of every color. Copy and cut out a candy box for each child. Divide your class into groups of three to five children that are at similar levels. Work with one group at a time, while the remaining students are working independently.

Teacher's Note: *When students have mastered the identification of the colors, begin to work on reading the color words. Use only white candy heart shapes and write a different color word on each one.*

Assessment

Give each child in your group several candy heart shapes and a candy box mat. Explain to the students that the object of the game is to place the correct color heart in the candy box. Verbally state a specific color, or use another means to come up with a color, such as, rolling a die or using a spinner that lands on the different colors. Give each child in the group several turns by playing the game two or three times. When each student selects the correct color several times, circle those colors on his or her assessment form.

Enrichment

In a resealable bag, send home the candy shapes, the candy box, and a copy of the directions below.

Directions: Play a color recognition game with your child. Ask your child to place the candy hearts on the candy box mat as you call out the specific color. Continue until all the colored hearts have been placed on the candy box. This game provides practice with color recognition.

Conversation Hearts Candy Patterns

Hug

You're Cute

Be Mine

Kiss Me

Sweetie

Love

Candy Box Mat

Directions: Copy and cut out for each child, the candy box pattern, to use with colored conversation heart shapes for assessment and enrichment. After assessment, send the candy box pattern, the colored conversation heart shapes, and a copy of the directions, home with the child for enrichment.

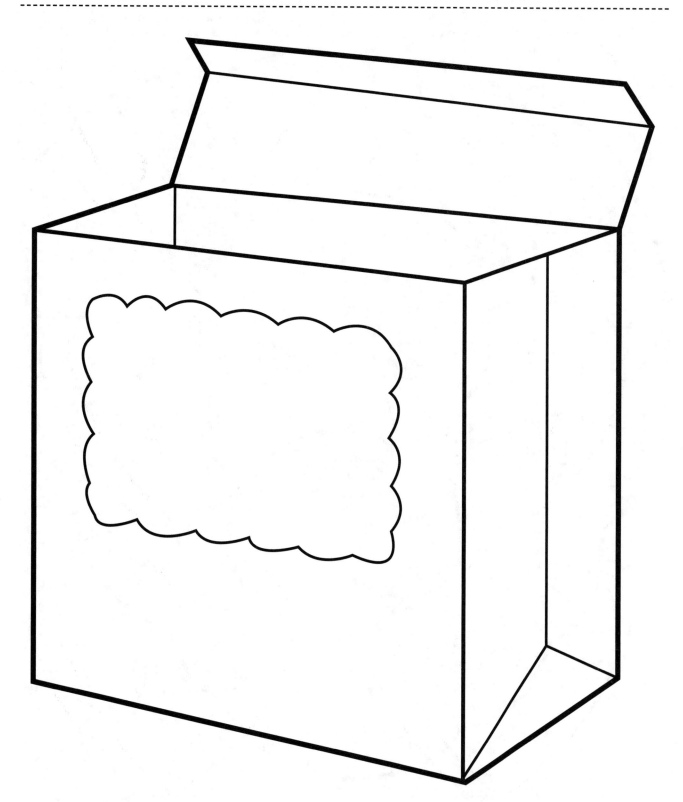

March

Lion's Mane Cutting Practice

Beginner

Directions: Copy and cut out a lion shape for each child. First have the children color the picture using crayons or markers. Next, ask the children to snip the short lines. Model for them how to scrunch the strips, or roll them around a pencil, to make them look like the lion's mane.

Leaping Lion Cutting Practice

Intermediate

Directions: Follow the leaping lion. Begin by placing your scissors on the stars. Cut along the paths and cut out the three boxes.

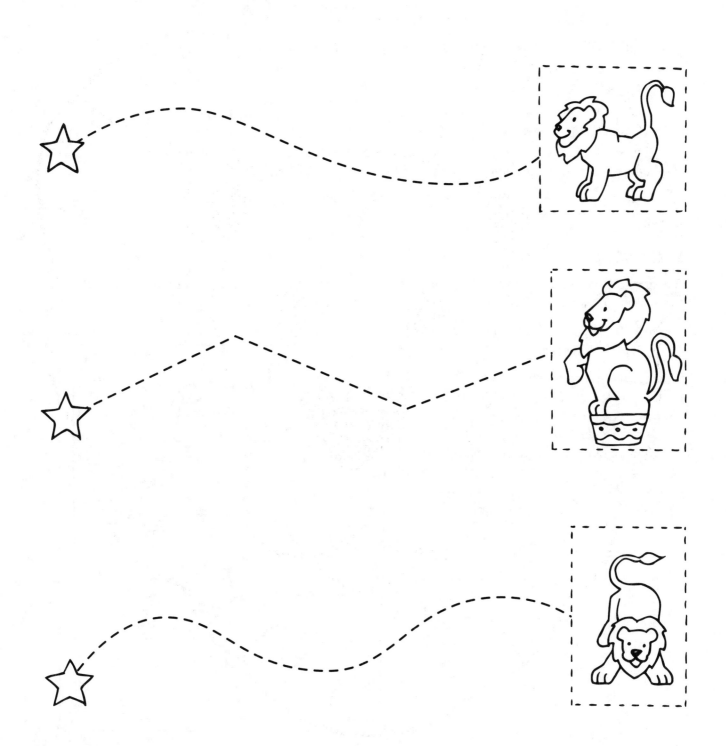

Lion's Main Cutting Activity

Materials

- Children's safety scissors
- Pencils
- Yellow construction paper
- Lion Face Patterns (page 74)
- Individual or Group Assessment Page (pages 143–144)

Procedure

1. Ask your students to trace their hands on pieces of yellow construction paper. Remind students to keep the hand that is on the paper still, and use the other hand to move the writing implement. For some children, it helps to put a little piece of rolled up tape on the underside of the construction paper during the tracing process to keep the paper from moving.

2. When your students have finished tracing their hands, provide scissors for them to cut out the tracings.

Assessment

Encourage children to show you the hands they cut out. Mark their skill levels on the appropriate form: *beginner, intermediate,* or *advanced.* Refer to the Cutting Skills on page 8 for guidelines.

Culminating Activity

Enlarge the lion face pattern (page 70) to fit the display area or bulletin board. Use yellow paper for the face and color the eyes black. Attach the lion face to the board and add the hand-shapes, facing all directions, around the lion's face, to represent the lion's mane. Curl or scrunch the fingers on the hands to add dimension.

Lion Face Color Identification

Materials

- Lion Face Patterns (page 74) in red, yellow, blue, green, orange, purple, pink, brown, black, and white for each child
- Lion Habitat Mat (page 75) traced or copied, for each child
- Resealable bag for each child
- Individual or Group Assessment Forms (pages 143–144)

Procedure

Copy and cut enough lion faces so that each child can have two of every color. Copy a lion habitat for each child. Divide the class into groups of three to five children who are at similar levels. Work with one group at a time, while the remaining students are working independently.

Teacher's Note: *When students have mastered identification of the colors, start working on reading the color words. Using only white lion shapes, write a different color word on each one.*

Assessment

Give each child a lion habitat and the colored lions he or she made. Explain that the object of the game is to place the correct color lion in the habitat. Verbally state a specific color, or use another means to come up with a color, such as, rolling a die or using a spinner that lands on the different colors. Give each child several turns by playing the game two or three times. When the child selects the correct color every time, record the results on his or her assessment form.

Enrichment

In a resealable bag, send home the colored lions, the habitat mat, and a copy of the directions below.

Directions: Play a game with your child. Ask your child to place the colored lions, and the habitat mat, on the floor in front of him or her. Ask your child to place the correct color lion on the habitat mat as you call out the specific color. Continue until all the colored lions have been placed on the habitat mat. This game provides practice with color recognition.

Lion Face Patterns

Lion Habitat Mat

Directions: Copy the lion habitat for each child to use with colored lion shapes for assessment and enrichment. After assessment, send the lion shapes and habitat home so each student can play the game with his or her parents.

Spring Counting Activities

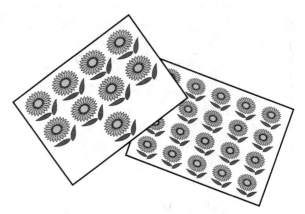

Materials

Spring Counting Cards (pages 77–80) for each student

Number Cards (pages 126–131) for each student

Resealable bag for each student

Individual or Group Assessment Forms (pages143–144)

Procedure

Begin with the picture cards. Have each member of the group lay the cards out on the floor. Ask the students to hold up a card displaying a certain number of objects. You can state a number, have each child take a turn to roll dice, or use a spinner that lands on the numbers you are testing. Start with small numbers and add larger numerals as the students progress. Make a note on each child's assessment form of the progress he or she is making. Assess number identification and number word identification in the same way.

> **Teacher's Note:** *Write the appropriate number on the back of each card for self checking. Use the assessment pages in April and May as well.*

Enrichment

Send home a resealable bag containing a set of number cards, a set of counting cards, and a copy of the directions below. Choose cards that are appropriate for each child's level.

Directions: Begin with the counting (picture) cards. Have your child lay the cards, face up, on the floor in front of him or her. Say a number and have your child pick up the card that displays that number of objects. Continue in this manner until all cards have been recognized. This game provides practice with counting. Next, work on number recognition and reading the number words.

3   three

Spring Counting Cards

March

Spring Counting Cards *(cont.)*

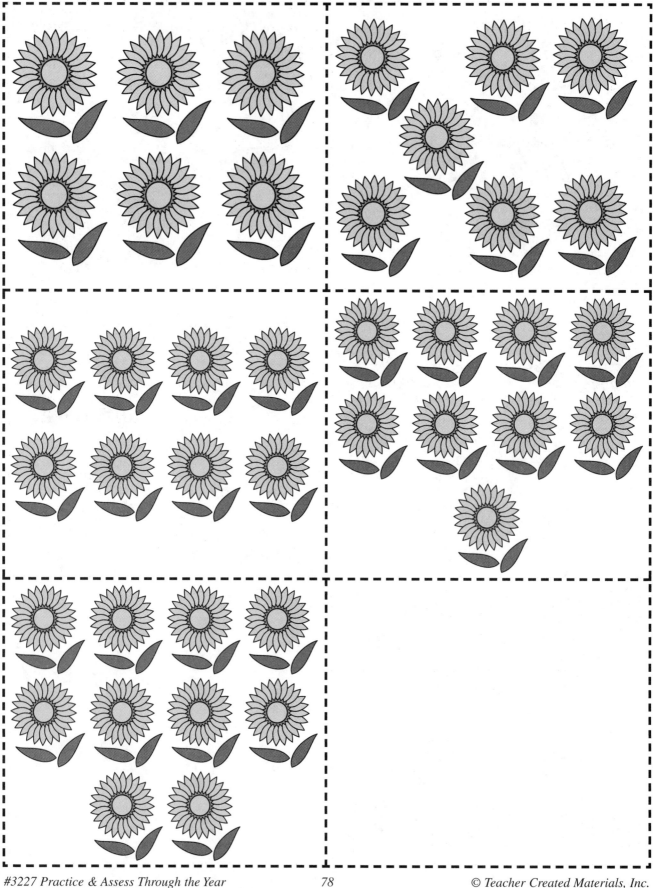

78   © Teacher Created Materials, Inc.

Spring Counting Cards *(cont.)*

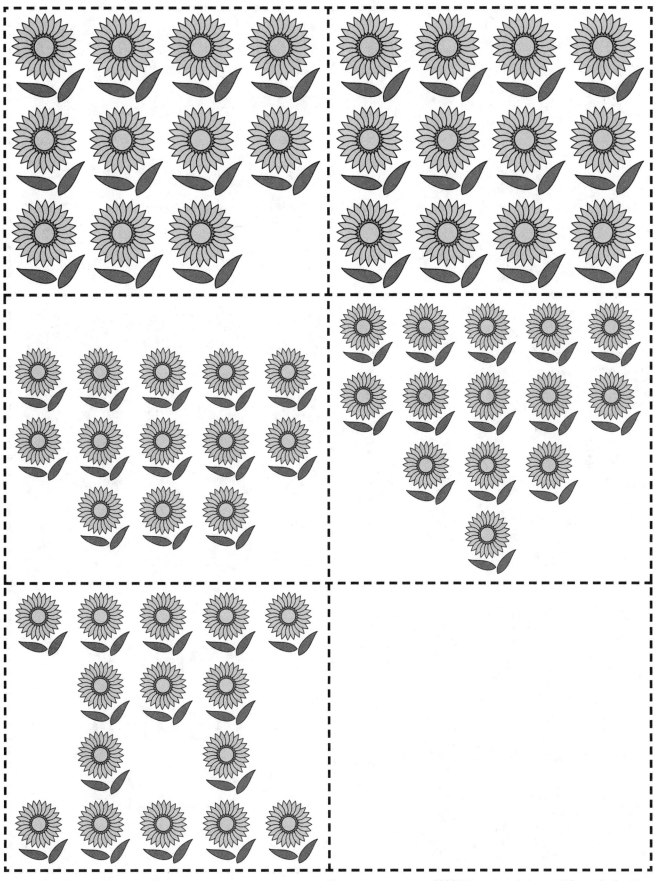

Spring Counting Cards *(cont.)*

Spring Alphabet Games

The Spring Alphabet Cards (pages 82–84) can be used in two ways, as game sheets or as flash cards. Directions for both are given below.

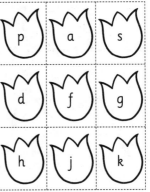

Game Sheets

Materials

- Spring Alphabet Cards page for each student
- Markers (beans, chips, paper clips, etc.)
- Resealable bag for each student
- Individual or Group Assessment Forms (pages 143–144)

Assessment

Give each child in a small group a set of spring alphabet pages. Decide ahead of time if they should do all three pages at once or do them one at a time. Call out a letter in random order, and have students find that letter on their sheets and cover them with a marker. This can be done as a whole group, or one at a time, giving each child a turn. Mark on the assessment form for each individual child, the letters he or she recognizes.

Flash Cards

Materials

- Spring Alphabet Cards for each student
- Resealable bag for each student
- Brown paper lunch sack for each student
- Individual or Group Assessment Forms (page 143–144)

Assessment

Mark on the assessment form for each individual child, the letters he or she recognizes when cards are shown.

Enrichment

Send home the appropriate Spring Alphabet Cards in a resealable bag. Enclose a copy of the direction card below and a brown paper lunch bag.

Raise It High Game

Ask your child to lay his or her cards on the floor in front of him or her. Name a letter of the alphabet (not in order) and ask him or her to find that card and hold it up in the air.

Letter Surprise Game

Give your child a lunch sack with the letter flash cards inside. Have him or her pull out a letter and name it. Continue until all the cards are gone.

Spring Alphabet Cards

Spring Alphabet Cards *(cont.)*

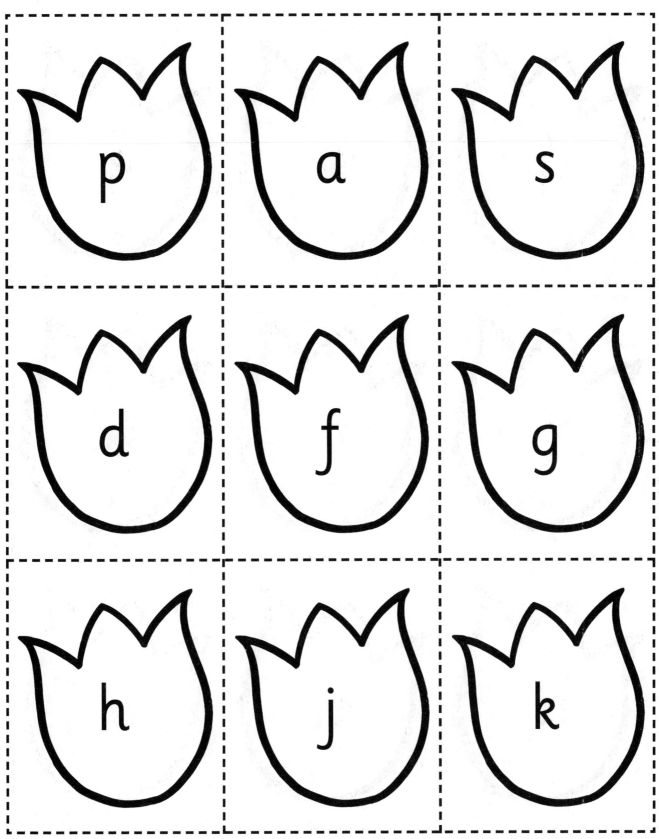

Spring Alphabet Cards *(cont.)*

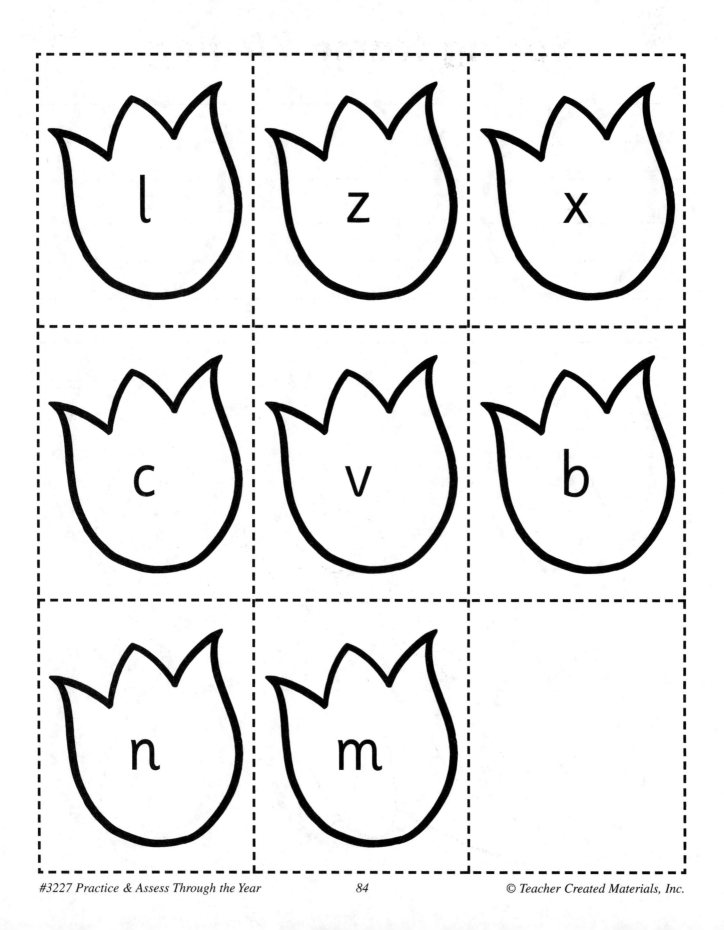

Spring Name Writing

☐ Yes ☐ No

Grass Cutting Practice

Beginner

Directions: Copy this page for each child. Fold the bottom of the paper over at the solid fold line. Have the children color the picture. Have your students use green to color part of the page that is folded over. Show them how to snip the folded edge so that it looks like grass.

Fold here

Butterfly Cutting Practice

Intermediate

Directions: Color and cut out the butterfly.

#3227 Practice & Assess Through the Year

Butterfly Cutting Activity

Materials

- Pencils
- Children's safety scissors
- Various colors construction paper
- Glue sticks
- Individual or Group Assessment Forms (pages 143–144)

Procedure

1. Using pencils, have children trace their hands, keeping their fingers close together, on a folded piece of construction paper. If cutting through two pieces of paper is too difficult, have your students trace their hands twice. Remind students to keep the hand that is on the paper still and use the other hand to move the pencil. For some children, it helps to put a little piece of rolled up tape on the underside of the construction paper while tracing to keep the paper from moving.

2. When your students have finished tracing their hands, provide scissors for them to cut out the tracings. They should have two hand shapes when they are finished.

3. Glue the two shapes to a new, larger, folded piece of construction paper with the thumb sides overlapping, to make a card.

4. Have the children cut the construction paper scraps into shapes to glue on the butterfly wings for decoration.

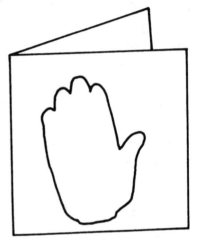

Assessment

Encourage each student to show you the hands he or she cut out. Mark his or her skill level on the appropriate form: *beginner, intermediate,* or *advanced.* Refer to the Cutting Skills on page 8 for guidelines.

Culminating Activity

Encourage each student to write a message to a parent, sibling, or friend inside his/her card. If necessary, have your students dictate a message while you write it in the card. Encourage your students to each write his/her name at the end of the message.

Butterfly Color Identification

Materials

- Butterfly Patterns (page 90) in red, yellow, blue, green, orange, purple, pink, brown, black, and white for each child
- Branch Pattern (page 91) copied and cut, one for each child
- Resealable bag for each child
- Individual or Group Assessment Forms (pages 143–144)

Procedure

Copy the butterflies on different colored paper. Cut out enough butterflies so that every child can have one of each color. Trace, cut, or copy a branch for each child. Use your judgment to divide the class into groups of three to five children who are at similar levels. Work with one group at a time, while the remaining students are working independently.

Teacher's Note: *When students have mastered identification of the colors, begin to work on reading the color words. Use only white butterfly shapes and write a different color name on each one.*

Assessment

Give each child a branch and the assortment of colored butterflies. Explain that the object of the game is to place the correct color butterfly on the branch. State a color, or have each child take a turn to roll a die, or use a spinner that lands on the specific colors on which you are working. Give each child several turns by playing the game two or three times. When a child has chosen a color correctly, circle the specific color on his or her assessment form.

Enrichment

In a resealable bag, send home the branch, the butterflies, and a copy of the directions below.

Directions: Play a color recognition game with your child. Ask your child to place the branch and the butterflies on the floor in front of him or her. As you call out a color, ask your child to find that color butterfly and place it on the branch. Continue calling out colors until all the colored butterflies have been placed on the branch. This game provides practice with color recognition.

Butterfly Patterns

Branch Pattern

Directions: Copy and cut out the branch pattern to use with the colored butterflies. When done with the assessment, send the butterfly and shapes home with the children.

Flower Petals Cutting Practice

Beginner

Directions: Copy and cut out a flower for each child. Ask the child to color the picture and then snip the short lines to produce a flower with petals.

Growing Vines Cutting Practice

Intermediate

Directions: Follow the growing vines. Begin at the stars, and using scissors, cut along the dotted lines. Cut out the three flowers at the end of the dotted lines.

Flower Cutting Activity

Materials

- Pencils
- Children's safety scissors
- Green and pastel colored construction paper
- Individual or Group Assessment Forms (pages 143–144)

Procedure

1. Have children place their hands, with the fingers open but thumb close to the side of the hand, on pastel pieces of construction paper. Ask your students to trace around their hands with a pencil. Remind them to keep the hand that is on the paper still and use the other hand to move the pencil. It helps to put a little piece of rolled up tape on the underside of the construction paper while tracing. This helps to keep the paper from moving.

2. When the students have finished tracing their hands, provide scissors for them to cut out their tracings.

Assessment

Encourage children to show you the hands they cut out. Mark their skill levels on the appropriate form: *beginner, intermediate,* or *advanced.* Refer to the Cutting Skills on page 8 for guidelines.

Culminating Activity

Cover a display area or bulletin board with blue at the top for sky, and green at the bottom for grass. Cut out stems and leaves, from green construction paper, for the children's hand-shaped flowers.

Attach the stems and leaves to the bulletin board and then add the "flowers." Encourage your students to verbally tell you where to put their flowers. Ask them to use directional words like *above, below,* and *beside.*

Flower Color Identification

Materials

- Flower Patterns (page 96) in red, yellow, blue, green, orange, purple, pink, brown, black, and white for each child
- Growing Stems Mat (page 97) traced or copied, for each child
- Resealable bag for each child
- Individual or Group Assessment Forms (pages 143–144)

Procedure

Copy and cut out enough flower shapes so that each child can have two of every color. Copy a growing stems mat for each child. Divide the class into groups of three to five children who are at similar levels. Work with one group at a time, while the remaining students are working independently.

Teacher's Note: *When students have mastered identification of the colors, begin to work on reading the color words. Use only white flower shapes and write a different color word on each one.*

Assessment

Give each child a growing stems mat and the assortment of colored flowers. Explain that the game is to place the correct color flower on the growing stems. You can state a color, or have each take a turn to roll a dice, or use a spinner that lands on the colors on which you are working. Give each child several turns by playing the game two or three times. When the child selects the correct color, circle the specific color on his or her assessment form.

Enrichment

In a resealable bag, send home the flowers, the growing stems mat, and a copy of the directions below.

Directions: Play a color recognition game with your child. Ask your child to place the flowers and the growing stems mat on the floor in front of him or her. As you call out a specific color, ask your child to find that color and place it on the growing stems mat. Continue calling out colors until all the colored flowers have been placed on the growing stems. This game provides practice with color recognition.

Flower Patterns

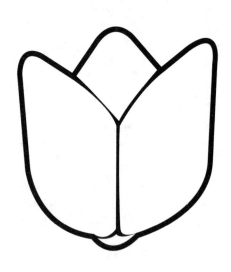

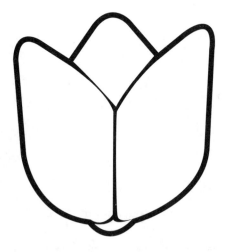
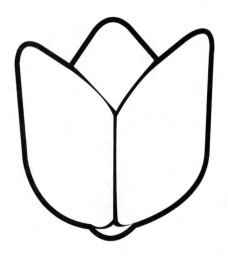

Growing Stems Mat

Seaweed Cutting Practice

Beginner

Directions: Copy this page for each child. Fold the bottom of the paper up at the solid fold line. Ask the students to color green the part of the page that is folded over, and then color the remainder of the picture in the colors of their choice. Model for your students how to use scissors to snip the folded edge so that it looks like seaweed.

Fold here

Fish Cutting Practice

Intermediate

Directions: Copy a picture of a fish for each student. Ask him or her to color and cut out the fish shape.

Fish Cutting Activity

Materials

- Pencils
- Children's safety scissors
- Assorted colors of construction paper
- Fish Bowl Mat (page 103)
- Assorted materials to decorate fish shape such as, glitter, sequins, and foil pieces.
- Glue sticks
- Individual or Group Assessment Forms (pages 143–144)

Procedure

1. Ask your students to trace their hands on their choices of construction paper. Have them hold their fingers tightly together and extend their thumbs to make a fin shape. Ask your students to use pencils to trace their hands. Remind students to keep the hand that is on the paper still and use the other hand to move the pencil. For some children it helps to put a little piece of rolled up tape on the underside of the construction paper during the tracing process to keep the paper from moving.

2. When your students have finished tracing their hands, provide scissors for them to cut out the tracings.

3. Make available an assortment of materials so students can decorate the fish they made.

Assessment

Encourage children to show you the fish they cut out. Mark their skill levels on the appropriate form: *beginner, intermediate,* or *advanced.* Refer to the Cutting Skills on page 8 for guidelines.

Culminating Activity

Enlarge the fish bowl pattern, on page 103, to fit the display area or bulletin board. Use blue paper to represent the water in the fish bowl, or lay the tracing on a large table or floor and have the students color or paint it.

Attach the fish bowl to the board and add the hand-shaped fish your students made. Encourage your students to verbally tell you where to put their fish in the bowl. Ask them to use directional words like *above, below,* and *beside.*

For a special effect, tape clear or light blue plastic wrap across the fish bowl after the students' fish have been attached. This will give the allusion of the fish and the water being inside a glass bowl.

Fish Color Identification

Materials

- Fish Patterns (page 102) in red, yellow, blue, green, orange, purple, pink, brown, black, and white, one of each for every child
- Fish Bowl Mat (page 103) traced, cut, or copied, for each child
- Resealable bag for each child
- Individual or Group Assessment Forms (pages 143–144)

Procedure

Cut enough fish shapes so that each child can have two of every color. Copy and cut out a fish bowl for each child. Divide the class into groups of three to five children that are at similar levels. Work with one group at a time, while the remaining students are working independently.

Teacher's Note: When students have mastered the identification of the colors, begin to work on reading the color words. Use only white fish shapes and write a different color word on each one.

Assessment

Give each child a fish bowl and their assortment of colored fish. Explain that the object of the game is to place the correct color fish on the fish bowl. State a color, or have each child take a turn rolling a colored die, or use a spinner that lands on the colors with which you are working. Give each child several turns by playing the game two or three times. When a child selects the correct color, circle the color on his or her assessment form.

Enrichment

In a resealable bag, send home the fish, the fish bowl mat, and a copy of the directions below.

Directions: Play a color recognition game with your child. Ask your child to place the fish and the fish bowl on the floor in front of him or her. As you call out a specific color, ask your child to find that color fish and place it on the fish bowl. Continue until all the colored fish have been placed on the fish bowl. This game provides practice with color recognition.

Fish Patterns

Fish Bowl Mat

Summer Counting Activity

Materials

- Summer Counting Cards (pages 105–108) for each student
- Number Cards (pages 126–131) for each student
- Resealable bag for each student
- Individual or Group Assessment Forms (pages 143–144)

Procedure

Begin by giving each child a set of the Counting cards. Ask your students to lay them out in front of them and ask them to show a card displaying a certain amount of objects. You can state a number, have each child take a turn rolling dice, or use a spinner that lands on the numbers on which you are working. Do this to practice the numbers that are appropriate for each group. Start with small numbers and add larger numerals as the students advance. Make a note on the assessment form of each student who can find and count the correct amount. Assess number identification and number word identification in the same way.

Teacher's Note: *Write the appropriate number on the back of each card for self-checking. Use these assessment pages in July and August as well.*

Enrichment

Send home with each student in a resealable bag, a set of number cards, a set of counting cards, and a copy of the directions below. Be sure to choose cards for each students that are appropriate for his or her level.

Directions: Play a counting game with your child. Begin with the counting (picture) cards. Ask your child to lay them on the floor in front of him or her. Say a specific number and have your child pick up the card with the same number of objects. Go through all the numbers in this manner. This activity provides practice in counting. Next, ask your child to identify specific numbers. Finally, help him or her read the number words.

Summer Counting Cards

Summer Counting Cards *(cont.)*

Summer Counting Cards (cont.)

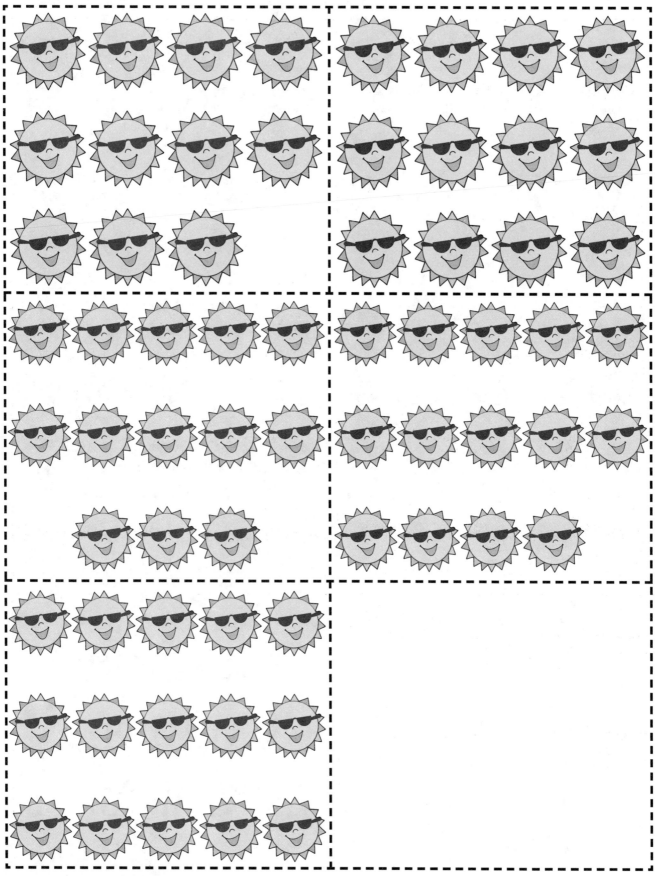

Summer Counting Cards *(cont.)*

Summer
Counting
Cards

108

Summer Alphabet Games

The Summer Alphabet Cards (pages 110–112) can be used in two ways, as game sheets or as flash cards. Directions for both are given below.

Game Sheets

Materials

- Summer Alphabet Cards page for each student (do not cut up)
- Markers (beans, chips, paper clips, etc.)
- Resealable bag for each student
- Individual or Group Assessment Forms (pages 143–144)

Assessment

Give each child in a small group a set of Summer Alphabet pages. Decide ahead of time if they should do all three pages at once or do them one at a time. Call out a letter in random order, and have students find that letter on their sheets and cover them with markers. This can be done as a whole group, or one at a time, giving each child a turn. Mark, on the assessment form for each individual child, the letters he or she recognizes.

Flash Cards

Materials

- Summer Alphabet Cards for each student
- Resealable bag for each student
- Brown paper lunch sack for each student
- Individual or Group Assessment Forms (page 143–144)

Assessment

Mark on the assessment form for each individual child, the letters he or she recognizes when cards are shown.

Enrichment

Send home the appropriate Summer Alphabet Cards in a resealable bag. Enclose a copy of the direction card below and a brown paper lunch bag.

Raise It High Game

Ask your child to lay his or her cards on the floor in front of him or her. Name a letter of the alphabet (not in order) and ask him or her to find that card and hold it up in the air.

Letter Surprise Game

Give your child a lunch sack with the letter flash cards inside. Have him or her pull out a letter and name it. Continue until all the cards are gone.

Summer Alphabet Cards

Summer Alphabet Cards (cont.)

Summer Alphabet Cards *(cont.)*

     112

Summer Name Writing

☐ Yes   ☐ No

Fireworks Cutting Practice

Beginner

Directions: Copy and cut out a fireworks shape for each child. Ask your students to snip the short lines to produce a showering fireworks effect.

Shooting Fireworks Cutting Practice

Intermediate

Directions: Follow the shooting fireworks. Start cutting at the stars and cut along the dotted lines.
Cut out the three showers of fireworks at the end of the dotted lines.

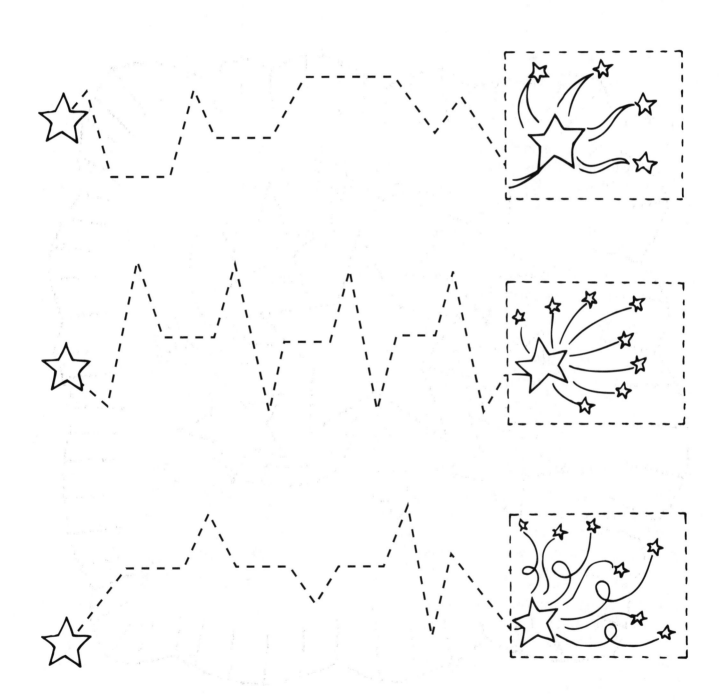

Sparkling Fireworks Cutting Activity

Materials

- Pencils
- Children's safety scissors
- White construction paper
- Glue
- Colored glitter
- Fireworks Pattern (page 118)
- Individual or Group Assessment Forms (pages 143–144)

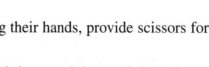

Procedure

1. Ask your children to trace their hands on pieces of white construction paper. Remind students to keep the hand that is on the paper still, and use their other hand to move the pencil. It helps to put a little piece of rolled up tape on the underside of the construction paper while tracing to keep the paper from moving.

2. When your students have finished tracing their hands, provide scissors for them to cut out the tracings.

3. Ask your students to put glue on the hand shape and then sprinkle glitter on the glue. Ask them to place the excess glitter in the trash can.

Assessment

Encourage children to show you the hands they cut out. Mark their skill levels on the appropriate form: *beginner, intermediate,* or *advanced.* Refer to the Cutting Skills on page 8 for guidelines.

Culminating Activity

Enlarge the fireworks pattern, making one firework red, one firework white, and one firework blue. Make them large enough to fit the display area or bulletin board. Attach the fireworks to the board.

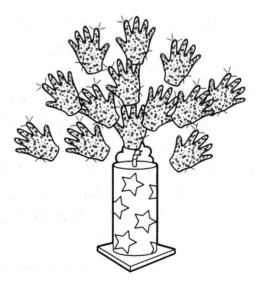

Add the hand shapes to represent the showering part of the fireworks. Encourage your students to verbally tell you where to put their hands. Ask them to use directional words like *above, below,* and *beside.*

Fireworks Color Identification

Materials

- Fireworks Patterns (page 118) in red, yellow, blue, green, orange, purple, pink, brown, black, and white for each child
- Fireworks Mat (page 119) traced, or copied, for each child
- Resealable bag for each child
- Individual or Group Assessment Forms (pages 143–144)

Procedure

Cut enough fireworks shapes so that each child can have two of every color. Trace, or copy, a fireworks mat for each child. Divide the class into groups of three to five children who are at similar levels. Work with one group at a time, while the remaining students are working independently.

> **Teacher's Note:** *When students have mastered identification of the colors, begin to work on reading the color words. Use only white firework shapes and write a different color name on each one.*

Assessment

Give each child a fireworks mat and his or her assortment of fireworks shapes. Explain that the object of the game is to place the correct color fireworks shape on the fireworks mat. Call out the name of a color for the students to find. Do this by naming a color, rolling a color die, or using a spinner that lands on the different colors. Give each child several turns by playing the game two or three times. When each child selects the correct color consistently, circle the specific colors on his or her assessment form.

Enrichment

Send home in a resealable bag with each student, the fireworks shapes, the fireworks mat, and a copy of the directions below.

Directions: Play a color recognition game with your child. Ask your child to place the fireworks shower shapes and fireworks mat on the floor in front of him or her. Name a specific color and ask your child to find that color firework and put it on the firework mat. Continue naming colors until all the colored shapes have been placed on the fireworks mat. This game provides practice in color recognition.

Fireworks Patterns

Fireworks Mat

Sun Rays Cutting Practice

Beginner

Directions: Copy and cut out a sun shape for each child. Ask your students to color the sun and snip the short lines to produce the effects of the shooting rays.

Sun Cutting Practice

Intermediate

Directions: Give each child a picture of the sun. Ask your students to color and cut out the sun.

Sun Rays Cutting Activity

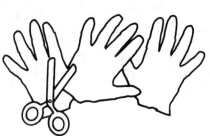

Materials

- Pencils
- Children's safety scissors
- Yellow construction paper
- Individual or Group Assessment Forms (pages 143–144)

Procedure

1. Ask your students to trace their hands on pieces of yellow construction paper. Remind students to keep the hand that is on the paper still, and use the other hand to move the pencil. It helps to put a little piece of rolled up tape on the underside of the construction paper to keep the paper from moving.

2. When your students have finished tracing their hands, provide scissors for them to cut out their tracings.

Assessment

Encourage children to show you the hands they traced. Mark their skill levels on the appropriate form: *beginner, intermediate,* or *advanced.* Refer to the Cutting Skills on page 8 for guidelines.

Culminating Activity

Make a large yellow circle and attach it to the center of a bulletin board. Use yellow paper, or lay the circle on a large table or floor and have the students color it. Draw a face on the circle to add character.

Attach the circle to the bulletin board and add the hand shapes around the circle to look like rays. Encourage your students to tell you where to put their hands. Ask them to use directional words like *above, below,* and *beside.*

Sun Shapes Color Identification

Materials

- Sun Patterns (page 124) in red, yellow, blue, green, orange, purple, pink, brown, black and white for each child
- Daytime Mat (page 125) traced or copied, for each child
- Resealable bag for each child
- Individual or Group Assessment Forms (pages 143–144)

Procedure

Copy and cut enough sun shapes so that each child can have two of every color. Trace or copy a daytime mat for each child. Divide the class into groups of three to five children who are at similar levels. Work with one group at a time, while the remaining students are working independently.

Teacher's Note: *When students have mastered identification of the colors, begin to work on reading the color words. Use only white sun shapes and write a different color name on each one.*

Assessment

Give each child a Daytime mat and their assortment of colored suns. Explain that the object of the game is to place the correct color sun onto the daytime mat. You can state a color, have each child take a turn rolling a colored dice, or use a spinner that lands on the colors on which you are working. Do this to practice the colors that are appropriate for each group. Give each child several turns by playing the game two or three times. When a child selects the correct color consistently, circle the specific colors on his or her assessment form.

Enrichment

In a resealable bag, send home colored sun shapes, the Daytime mat, and a copy of the directions below.

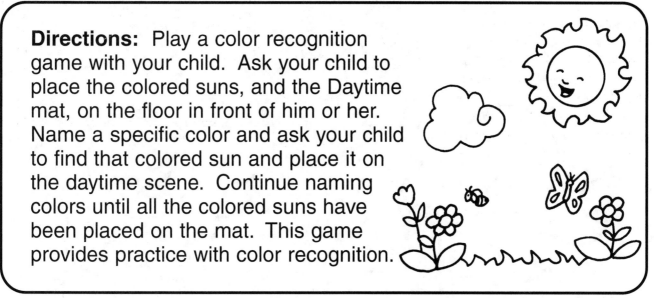

Directions: Play a color recognition game with your child. Ask your child to place the colored suns, and the Daytime mat, on the floor in front of him or her. Name a specific color and ask your child to find that colored sun and place it on the daytime scene. Continue naming colors until all the colored suns have been placed on the mat. This game provides practice with color recognition.

Sun Patterns

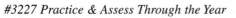

Daytime Mat

Number Book or Cards

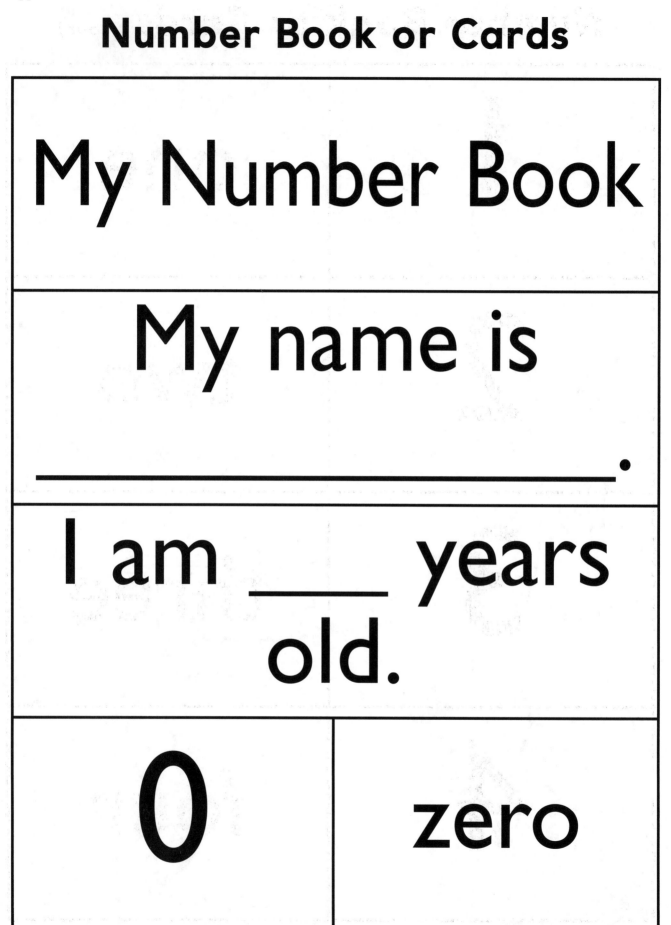

My Number Book

My name is

_____.

I am ____ years old.

| 0 | zero |

Number Book or Cards *(cont.)*

1	one
2	two
3	three
4	four

Number Book or Cards *(cont.)*

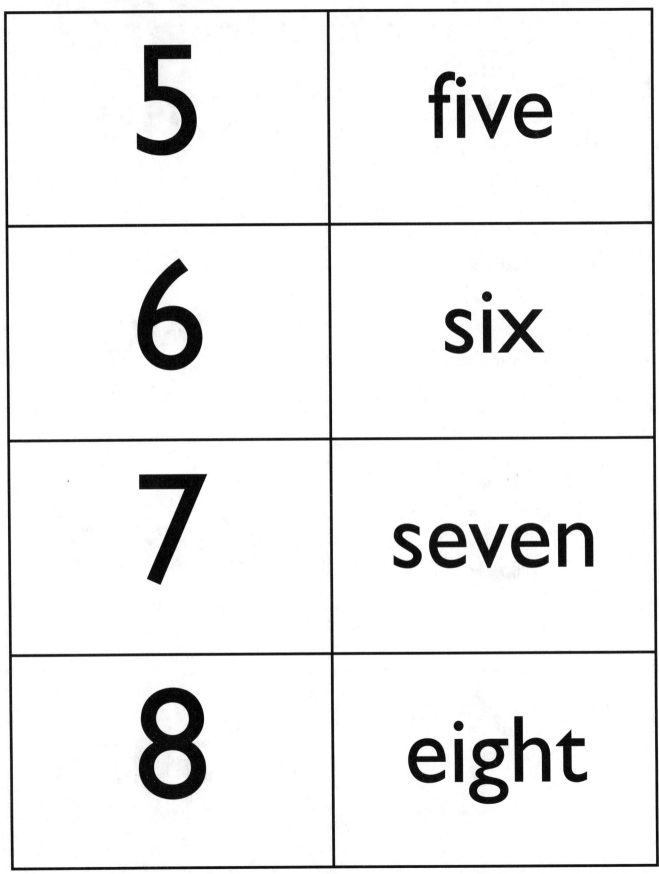

5	**five**
6	**six**
7	**seven**
8	**eight**

Number Book or Cards *(cont.)*

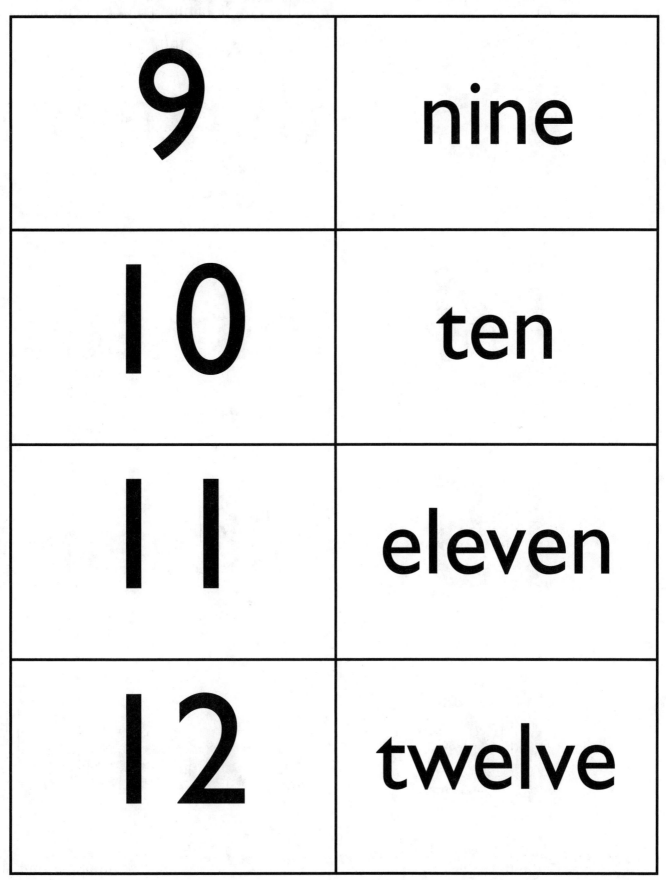

9	nine
10	ten
11	eleven
12	twelve

Number Book or Cards *(cont.)*

13	thirteen
14	fourteen
15	fifteen
16	sixteen

Number Book or Cards *(cont.)*

17	seventeen
18	eighteen
19	nineteen
20	twenty

Alphabet Book or Cards

My Alphabet
Book

A   a

B   b

Alphabet Book or Cards *(cont.)*

Alphabet Book or Cards *(cont.)*

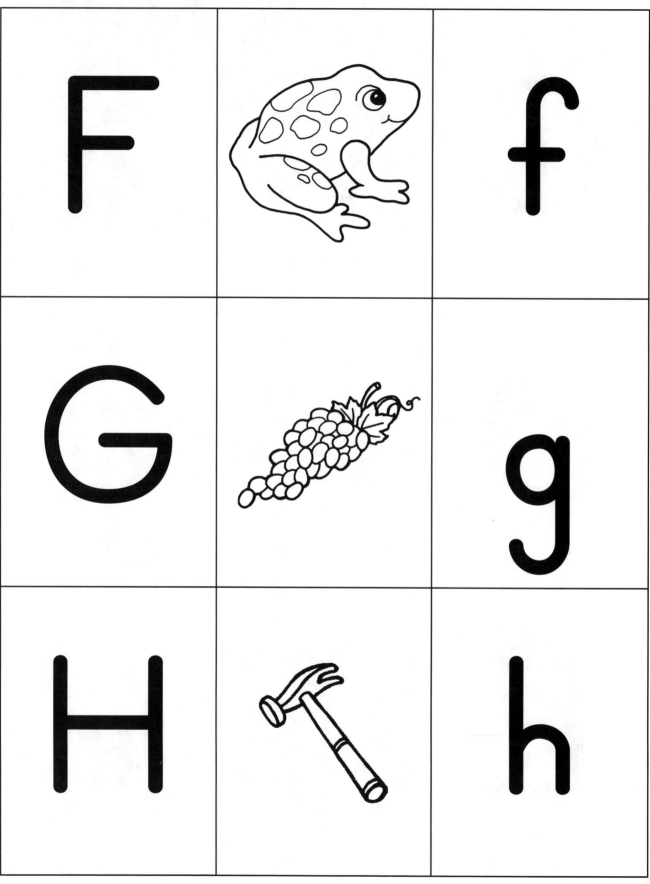

Alphabet Book or Cards *(cont.)*

Alphabet Book or Cards (cont.)

Alphabet Book or Cards *(cont.)*

Alphabet Book or Cards (cont.)

Alphabet Book or Cards *(cont.)*

U   u

V   v

W   w

Alphabet Book or Cards (cont.)

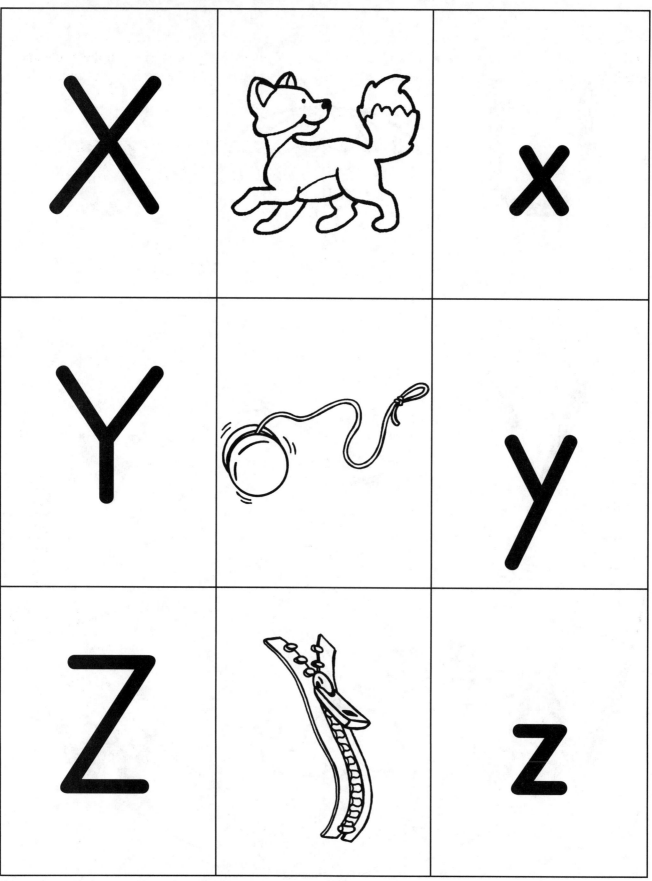

Color Spinner

Directions: Copy the circle and the arrow onto cardstock paper or cardboard for each child. Ask your students to use crayons or felt pens to color each section the appropriate color. Cut out the circle and attach the arrow to the center of the circle with a metal fastener. Laminate each piece for durability.

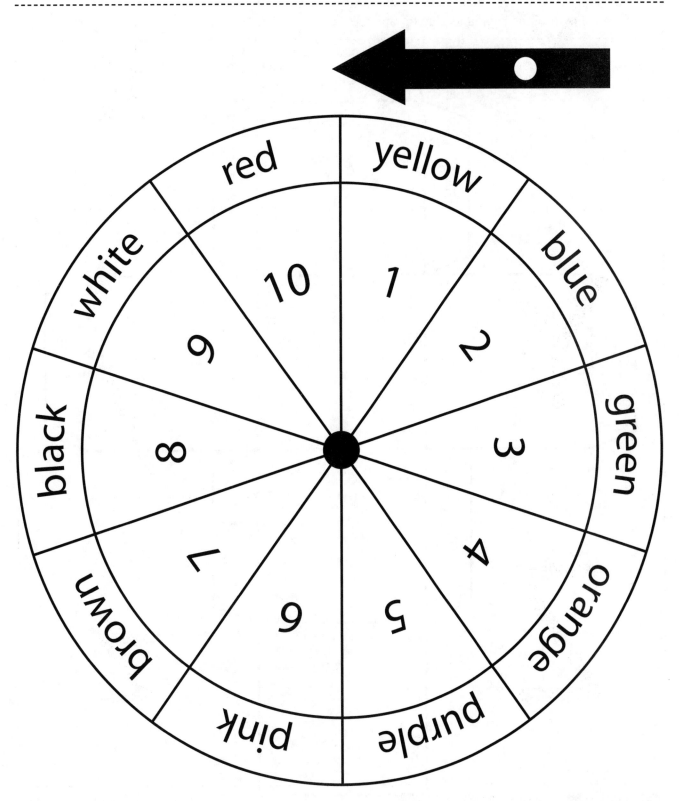

Color Cube

Directions: Copy the cube pattern onto cardstock paper or cardboard. Ask your students to use crayons to color each square a different color or write the appropriate numbers in each square. Cover the pattern with clear shelf paper, if durability is desired. Fold the cube as shown to the right and glue or tape the sides together.

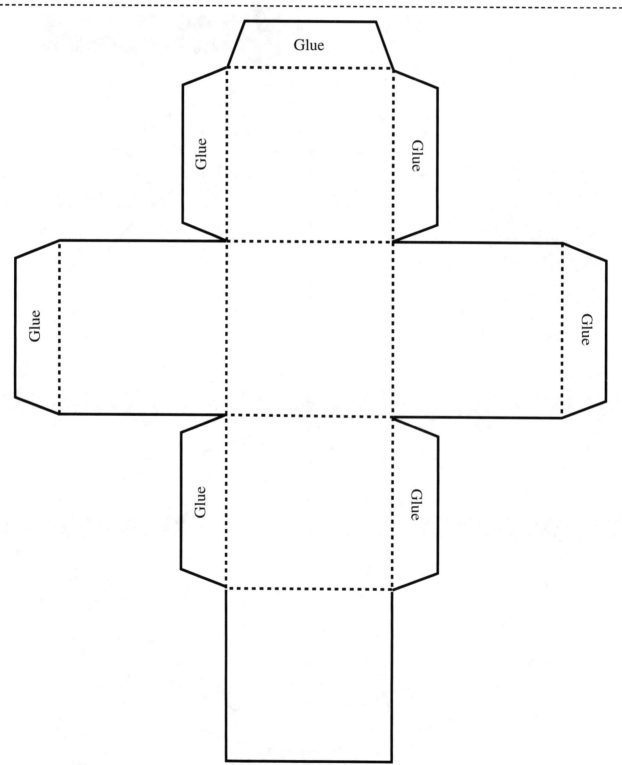

Individual Assessment Form

Name _____ Date_____

1. Cutting

☐	☐	☐
Beginner (needs work)	**Intermediate** (improving)	**Advanced** (mastered)

2. Colors (Check all colors identified.)

❏ Red	❏ Green	❏ Brown
❏ Blue	❏ Orange	❏ White
❏ Yellow	❏ Purple	❏ Black

3. Counting and Number Recognition (Mark with X when the skill is accomplished.)

Numbers	0–5	6–10	11–15	16–20	above
Can count					
Can identify numerals					
Can identify number words					

4. Alphabet Recognition (Circle all recognized letters.)

Uppercase

A	B	C	D	E	F	G
H	I	J	K	L	M	N
O	P	Q	R	S	T	U
V	W	X	Y	Z		

Lowercase

a	b	c	d	e	f	g
h	i	j	k	l	m	n
o	p	q	r	s	t	u
v	w	x	y	z		

5. Name Recognition

Recognizes First Name [yes] [no]   Recognizes Last Name [yes] [no]

Writes First Name [yes] [no]   Writes Last Name [yes] [no]

Group Assessment Form

Name	Assessment	Writes First Name	Writes Last Name	Knows Colors	Beg. Cutting	Int. Cutting	Adv. Cutting	Uppercase Alphabet	Lowercase Alphabet	Numbers 1–5	Numbers 6–10	Numbers 11–15	Numbers 16–20